# Evaluation Failures

Sara Miller McCune founded SAGE Publishing in 1965 to support the dissemination of usable knowledge and educate a global community. SAGE publishes more than 1000 journals and over 800 new books each year, spanning a wide range of subject areas. Our growing selection of library products includes archives, data, case studies and video. SAGE remains majority owned by our founder and after her lifetime will become owned by a charitable trust that secures the company's continued independence.

Los Angeles | London | New Delhi | Singapore | Washington DC | Melbourne

# Evaluation Failures

## 22 Tales of Mistakes Made and Lessons Learned

**Foreword by Michael Quinn Patton**

**Kylie Hutchinson**

Editor

Los Angeles | London | New Delhi
Singapore | Washington DC | Melbourne

FOR INFORMATION:

SAGE Publications, Inc.
2455 Teller Road
Thousand Oaks, California 91320
E-mail: order@sagepub.com

SAGE Publications Ltd.
1 Oliver's Yard
55 City Road
London EC1Y 1SP
United Kingdom

SAGE Publications India Pvt. Ltd.
B 1/I 1 Mohan Cooperative Industrial Area
Mathura Road, New Delhi 110 044
India

SAGE Publications Asia-Pacific Pte. Ltd.
3 Church Street
#10-04 Samsung Hub
Singapore 049483

Acquisitions Editor:   Helen Salmon
Editorial Assistant:   Megan O'Heffernan
Production Editor:   Jane Martinez
Copy Editor:   Colleen Brennan
Typesetter:   C&M Digitals (P) Ltd.
Proofreader:   Sally Jaskold
Cover Designer:   Ginkhan Siam
Marketing Manager:   Susannah Goldes

Printed in the United States of America

*Library of Congress Cataloging-in-Publication Data*

Names: Hutchinson, Kylie, editor.

Title: Evaluation failures : 22 tales of mistakes made and lessons learned / Kylie Hutchinson, editor.

Description: Thousand Oaks : SAGE Publications, [2018]

Identifiers: LCCN 2018021805 | ISBN 9781544320007 (pbk. : alk. paper)

Subjects: LCSH: Evaluation research (Social action programs) | Social sciences—Methodology.

Classification: LCC H62 .E84727 2018 | DDC 001.4—dc23
LC record available at https://lccn.loc.gov/2018021805

This book is printed on acid-free paper.

**MIX**
Paper from
responsible sources
FSC® C008955
www.fsc.org

18 19 20 21 22 10 9 8 7 6 5 4 3 2 1

# CONTENTS

# FOREWORD

## No Success Like Failure

Michael Quinn Patton
*Utilization-Focused Evaluation*

Spoiler alert! This book is about *evaluators'* failures. Not evaluation failures. Not "blame the victim" type failures—oh, those incompetent, unappreciative, and lacking-in-insight stakeholders. Not the failures of politicians, bureaucrats, funders, program staff, community members, or even program participants to be open to, understand, pay attention to, revel in the wonders of, and use evaluation. Unsavory stakeholders and hard-to-deal-with characters do, indeed, appear in these stories, but difficult people come with the territory and dealing with them is part of the job. These evaluators acknowledge that they failed to adequately do so in the evaluations recounted herein. These personal stories of evaluators failing epitomize *reflective practice* at the highest level.

The result of their collective honesty, bravery, forthrightness, and integrity are important and insightful lessons. Whatever your evaluation status, approach, position, expertise, or longevity, you can learn from these lessons. What makes these lessons all the more trustworthy, meaningful, and perceptive is that they come from highly successful evaluators. These are experienced, knowledgeable, accomplished, and highly competent evaluators. They believe in and care about evaluation. They are dedicated, career evaluation professionals. I know most of them personally. I would not hesitate to recommend any one of them. And yet they have all failed at some point. Which is part of the reason I have confidence in them. They can recognize, acknowledge, and own failure. They've been there, done that. Because they are successful, value success, strive for success, and consistently achieve success, they know failure when they see it, experience it, cause it, and feel it. Yes, especially, feel it. As the contributors say in the following chapters:

- "I was so shocked I could not breathe."

- "I felt incredibly embarrassed and disappointed."

- "I cringe when I think back about this."

- "I left the meeting with a hollow feeling in the pit of my stomach."

- "My fears quickly became reality."

- "I may have actually shed tears over this one. I was devastated."

- "There are days I feel like a total imposter, like my résumé is one failure after another and the whole world knows it."

What generated such feelings?

- It was "the evaluation from hell."

- "We were trying to turn straw into gold, but we did not have any magic to make it happen."

- "I could not believe that, so close to completion and despite all its flaws, this wonderful project was being snatched from me. Why hadn't I seen this coming? Where were the fault lines? What false assumptions had I made?"

- ". . . as a young evaluator, I was often part of the problem."

- It was a "scope creep train wreck."

- "How did we miss all the red flags?"

- "Furious stakeholder yelling . . ."

- "Change was everywhere."

- "My failure was continuing a path of poor decisions."

- "We failed terribly."

- "All hell broke loose, not catastrophically, but little by little, and it all added up."

- ". . . the cumulative snowball effect—how a flurry of relatively minor challenges could pile up and leave me feeling overwhelmed and unable to solve it."

- "Sometimes the stars in our eyes get in the way of being able to clearly see red flags that are there from the start."

- "The department finally took the bull by the horns and sent an emissary to my office to terminate the project."

## A Wide Range of Challenges Contributed to These Failures

The challenges faced by these evaluators, in combination and taken as a whole, read like a checklist for what you ought to be ready to face in most any evaluation. These challenges include design issues, data collection problems, political dynamics, difficult relationships, contextual complexities, turnover of key people, delays, communications issues, data access problems, weak administrative arrangements, incorrect assumptions, tough negotiations, diverse perspectives, cross-cultural misunderstandings, conflicting agendas in commissioning evaluations, and lack of program capacity. Cutting across and through these challenges, in every case, was the failure of the evaluator to fully recognize the extent and nature of the challenge, analyze the situation, and take timely action.

Been there, done all of that.

## Difficult Circumstances

Some years ago at an American Evaluation Association (AEA) conference, there was a T-shirt slogan/bumper sticker contest. The winning entry was "Evaluators do IT under difficult circumstances."

In this book, you'll have the pleasure of reading about others' (as opposed to your own) failures: presentation failures; failure to understand context; failure to listen; failure to manage expectations; communication failures; methodological miscalculations; interpersonal conflicts; misunderstandings, miscommunications, and relationship problems with key stakeholders; an inaccurate logic model; problems with data collection field workers; hassles with evaluation colleagues; and reporting missteps. Not all of these tales are full-blown failures per se. In many cases they're simply mistakes or a series of challenges that made the evaluation feel like a failure for the evaluator. These mistakes are not sugar-coated. A special edition of the *Canadian Journal of Program Evaluation* (Patton, 2010) reported stories of "how to take advantage of experience with evaluation that cannot be described as successful" (p. 151). No such euphemisms here. Taken together, these chapters constitute a collection of evaluation failures, plain and simple—no sugar-coating.

In publicly sharing these failures, evaluators join a major movement in our times to openly acknowledge failure, all the better to learn from them and share those learnings. Engineers Without Borders attracted a lot of amazed attention when the organization issued their first *Failure Report* in 2012; it has issued an annual failure report every year since then. Other organizations have similarly embraced failure in a very public way. FailForward has created a website and facilitated processes for "admitting failure" (www.admitting failure.org). Fail Festivals for sharing failures ("the f-word") are being held around the world (www.failfestival.org). The theme these initiatives share is that failure happens. But it's only really a failure if no learning occurs. So, *fail often, fail fast, and learn much.*

In a book titled *Adapt: Why Success Always Starts with Failure,* Tim Harford (2011) draws on a broad range of both historical and contemporary examples to illustrate the need for making more effective use of failures. He argues for the importance of systematically learning from trial and error, and building success through adaptation based on learning from reflection on failures.

In my view, the predominant lesson in this volume's cases is the importance of ongoing situation analysis and adaptation as an evaluation unfolds from early negotiations about focus through methods decisions and data collection through to reporting and follow-up for use. Learning from failures of the kind offered in these pages is essential to evaluation's future long-term success as a profession.

## Speaking Truth to Each Other

In 2015, the theme of the annual AEA conference was Exemplary Evaluations in a Multicultural World: Learning From Evaluation's Successes. To bring some balance to the theme, I proposed and chaired a session on Learning From Failure, featuring a presentation by Stephanie Evergreen, one of the contributors to this volume. So, there were some 500 sessions on success and one on failure. The session attracted a large crowd and included opportunities for audience members to share their stories of failures. Stephanie and I repeated the session in 2016 to an even larger audience. In addition to Stephanie, the 2017 session featured this book's editor, Kylie Hutchinson, and another of this book's contributors, Rakesh Mohan. What we found in offering these Learning From Failure sessions at AEA is that people are hungry for learning and eager to do so on a foundation of honesty about both successes and failures. We have received feedback from many colleagues expressing appreciation and gratitude for the AEA Learning From Failure sessions, and reports of being inspired to acknowledge, reflect on, and share their own failures. This collection of failure stories will surely build that momentum. Kudos to all of the contributors. Thank you for sharing.

The theme of the 2018 AEA conference was Speaking Truth to Power. Sharing failures involves speaking truth to each other. Speaking truth to each other may well be a prerequisite for effectively and credibly speaking truth to power.

## How to Read These Stories

I noted earlier that these stories of failure all conclude with lessons. Many of you will, I suspect, be inclined to turn to the end of each chapter and read just the lessons, skipping the case details that yielded the lessons. Let me offer an alternative approach. Read each case in full and before reading the author's reported lessons, identify the lessons that **you** take from the case.

Immerse yourself in each story. Be present to what unfolds. Put yourself in the situation being described. Follow the story's twists and turns. Imagine that you are making the decisions that have to be made. Think about the adaptations conceived and implemented. How would you have responded in a similar situation? What additional options might you consider? Reflect on each case in depth. That's how you learn from cases. Not by skimming them. Certainly not by skipping the details and rushing forward to the concluding lessons. You learn by savoring each case. Drink deeply of the details. Spend time with these extraordinary evaluation colleagues. Give yourself up to their stories. Your evaluation colleagues are talking to you. Be present and mindful. Don't fail to take full advantage of the learning opportunity of each case.

Finally, I would offer this. To provide a consistent theme of inquiry across the cases, as you read these cases, ponder and reflect on 2016 Nobel Laureate Bob Dylan's lyrics from "Love Minus Zero/No Limit":

There's no success like failure,
And failure's no success at all.

# REFERENCES

Engineers Without Borders. (2012). *Failure report 2012*. Retrieved from https://www.ewb.ca/wp-content/uploads/2016/12/2012_EWB_Failure_Report.pdf

Patton, M. Q. (2010). Incomplete successes. *The Canadian Journal of Program Evaluation, 25*(3), 151–163.

# ACKNOWLEDGMENTS

I would like to thank all the contributors to this book for their time and honesty. Thanks also to the advance reviewers for their comments and feedback: Linda Peritz, Graham Shaw, Sandra Sellick, and Kate McLeod. I am also grateful for the feedback from the SAGE reviewers, which helped develop this project:

Sonya Dublin, *University of California, Berkeley School of Public Health*

Leslie A. Fierro, *Claremont Graduate University*

Marcus-Antonio Galeste, *Arizona State University*

Amanda Olejarski, *West Chester University*

Beverly Peters, *American University*

Robert Renaud, *University of Manitoba*

Sandra Schrouder, *Barry University*

Thank you to Helen Salmon and SAGE Publishing for shepherding this project to completion. Special thanks to Anita Myers for introducing me to evaluation thirty years ago. And finally, thank you to Michael and Lucy for tolerating yet another book.

# INTRODUCTION

I remember my first evaluation failure. Before the days of electronic PDFs, I sent a hard copy of a final report by special courier to a client to meet their urgent deadline. The evaluation had been particularly interesting and I was excited about the results and recommendations presented in the report. Then I heard nothing from the client for several weeks. It turns out my report sat in their mail room with nobody bothering to look for it. Clearly, it was not "urgent," and I began to get concerned that they might ignore the valuable findings within it.

Unfortunately, during a subsequent phone call with the client, the client misinterpreted my excitement about the contents of the report as an ownership issue. All I wanted was for them not to ignore the results, but they thought I was telling them what to do with the report. An hour later I received a terse email from the client stating that the results were theirs to do with as they wished and that my role in the evaluation was finished. I was devastated. I took to my bed for at least a day, maybe more. Several weeks later, we met for coffee and cleared everything up. To this day, I'm still convinced I could have avoided the whole situation if we had initially talked in person rather than over email or the phone.

But it was months and even years before I felt I could tell anyone. At first, I only told friends outside the evaluation profession. I'm grateful for all the unconditional positive regard they gave me, which I desperately needed at the time. Then a funny thing happened. As time went by, my shame got less and less, to the point where I was comfortable sharing with other evaluators. That's the thing with screw-ups; the farther away you move from them, the less awful they become. And what remains after all the tears, hugs, hiding in bed, and empty bottles of wine, is the learning.

We can keep this learning to ourselves, or we can choose to share it with others when we're ready. Because whatever you call them—mistakes, goofs, slip-ups, or whatever—we will all experience some form of failure in our career at some point. A friend of mine once referred to these failures as AFOG: Another F-ing Opportunity for Growth. I think that's an apt phrase because it's how we reflect and grow as a result of our mistakes that counts. And if we can't learn from our own failures as evaluators, how can we expect our stakeholders to?

Reflective practice is necessary to be a good evaluator, but, sometimes, it's hard to create the space for this to happen. An important first step is giving ourselves permission to fail, which is the intent of this book. What follows are twenty-two tales told by evaluators who have messed up, come out the other side, and are ready to share their learning with you.

It was shockingly easy to find contributors for this book. I started out by first approaching well-known names in evaluation and then asking other highly experienced colleagues. I did this intentionally to demonstrate that failure strikes all of us equally at any time; age and experience can't necessarily protect us. In fact, many contributors have recounted mistakes that happened to them only recently. One thing that age and experience might enable, however, is a greater resiliency to weather failure when it happens. Perhaps it's the years of accumulated mistakes and the passage of time that allow us to accept our fallibility as evaluators more readily. This leads to personal forgiveness, laughter, and the ability to share our mistakes with others. Note that not all of these tales are full-blown failures. In many cases they're simply mistakes or slip-ups that presented a challenge for the evaluator.

I found it very validating while editing these chapters to know that I'm not the only one who has stumbled. Nor am I the only one with a tendency to ignore my successes and focus on the failures. But it's important to note that there are many, many successes in evaluation every day. My favourite part of being an evaluator is when I'm able to identify that one finding, conclusion, or recommendation that I know can really make a difference to a program or organization. And, frankly, this happens a lot.

I am sincerely grateful to all my colleagues who contributed to this book for their bravery and candidness in sharing. I've tried to select a wide range of stories that represent the experience of both internal and external evaluators in different sectors. If you're an internal evaluator without clients per se, you will still find most of the lessons applicable and vice versa. I've also arranged the stories to cover the generic evaluation process, from engaging stakeholders to ensuring use. Note that in some chapters, the author has altered certain story details so the focus remains on the evaluation failure and not the specific actors or program involved.

That's all I'm going to say at this point because I know you're eager to see how we all messed up and learn vicariously from our mistakes. Please do!

Kylie Hutchinson
Editor

# IT'S NOT ME, IT'S YOU

## The Value of Addressing Conflict Head On

### Corey Newhouse

*Corey Newhouse, MPP, is the founder and principal of Public Profit, an evaluation consultancy that helps mission-driven organizations measure and manage what matters.*

t's tough to predict the day that you'll lose your largest client. Like so many things, it's obvious to me now, but I sure didn't see it coming that day. Losing a quarter of my company's revenue in half an hour hurt. It hurt a lot. The good news is that our company is still standing, and we've learned a lot from the mistakes that culminated in the failure I'm about to describe.

## ABOUT ME

I have been a professional evaluator since 2003, primarily as an external consultant. I founded Public Profit in 2007; we help mission-driven organizations use data to improve the quality of their services to the community. Over the course of my career I've had the good fortune to work with organizations ranging from policy advocates to museums, foundations, and schools. I love helping our clients learn to use data to improve.

In this chapter, I share how I learned to approach conflict with clients directly and constructively. Although I write from the perspective of an external evaluation consultant, the lessons can apply to any situation in which an evaluator is working in service to another team.

## DESCRIPTION OF THE EVALUATION

Because we are a small consulting firm, our growth is directly tied to the size and duration of our projects, and there's often stiff competition for the most lucrative contracts. We were therefore thrilled to be selected to evaluate a large portfolio of youth programs supported by a major funder, both because it offered a chance to use a variety of methods and because it vastly improved our bottom line.

The evaluation itself was sweeping in scope; it included more than 100 program sites among dozens of grantees that were funded to do everything from sports leagues to arts programming to summer camps. The client, which funded the programs, was interested in traditional monitoring metrics, like program enrollment and attendance figures, and also gave us substantial latitude to craft an evaluation that explored their grantee portfolio. In response, we created a mixed methods evaluation design that incorporated multiple surveys, structured program observations, focus groups, case studies, and interviews. Because the portfolio was so large, we essentially conducted three separate evaluation studies, each aligned with a different funding strategy. As the external evaluator, we were responsible for orienting grantees to the project, collecting most of the data, and producing reports for a variety of audiences.

The first year of the project was pretty great. We got to know the many terrific organizations in the grant portfolio, collected tons of useful data, and created a variety of written reports that were (eventually) well received by the client. As with any new client, we learned about their quirks, too. For example, although we worked directly with our client's evaluation manager, the client instituted an extensive review process for the evaluation involving multiple people for nearly every part of the project, which we didn't anticipate when building our budget and work plan. This feedback from multiple people was often contradictory, making it difficult to understand what to do next. Resolving these contradictory requests required even more of our time. In addition, the client was fond of old school reporting methods, which we learned primarily by receiving negative feedback to early report drafts, which our client felt were too "pretty" to be taken seriously.

We're most effective when we flex our approach to meet the needs of our clients, so we did our best to adjust in the first year. Yet, we grumbled about it internally, bemoaning their bureaucratic ways and strategizing about how to nudge them into being more timely and consistent with their input. We also sought ways to convince them to modernize their approach to reporting, frequently forwarding blog posts and articles on the topic.

We overran our first year's project budget by about 50%. These overruns were due to our "just say yes" approach for a lucrative project, along with the extra time needed to navigate the lengthy review process. And although I was pleased with the quality of our work in the first year, as a business owner I knew that we had to buckle down on cost management to make this work. I asked our team to really hold the line in the second year of the project, agreeing to add components to the evaluation only if others were taken out.

With the benefit of hindsight, I now realize there were three issues that affected the project in the second year:

- Our internal grumbling didn't always stay inside the office. Our frustrations with the funder's evaluation manager sometimes bubbled over into our interactions, whether via email or during in-person meetings.

- The contradictory input from the evaluation manager and other staff members in the foundation about our work reflected deeper organizational disagreements about the purpose of our evaluation. These disagreements remained unresolved.

- Our major cost overruns in Year 1 required much stronger budget management in Year 2. We didn't make this decision crystal clear to the evaluation manager.

## THE MISTAKE OR CHALLENGE

In the second year of the project, the evaluation manager was on extended leave, so we developed a scope of work with another member of the organization. Our temporary point of contact mentioned that we'd need to be flexible with the evaluation, since the evaluation manager would want to make some changes upon their return. I figured this meant we'd need to update some data collection tools and swap out a few focus groups for interviews, but honestly, my thoughts at the time were much more focused on how to stay within budget. I didn't really push to understand what "be flexible" meant at the time.

Once back on the job, the evaluation manager began asking our team fundamental questions about our approach, ranging from whether we could include additional stakeholder interviews for one of the sub-studies, to making substantial changes to the content and timing of data collection tools that we already considered final. These requests were annoying for our team, as it felt like we were being second-guessed every step of the way. And in keeping with the "no new tasks" mandate, our team sought to find other ways to cut back so that we could stay within budget. These negotiations were often tense, and more than once the evaluation manager mentioned feeling shortchanged.

Our grumbling intensified as the second year progressed, because the evaluation manager seemed to be acting ever more unpredictably and unfairly. From our point of view, we kept receiving major, last-minute change requests from the evaluation manager, with little appreciation for how challenging—and time-consuming—it was to make major mid-course adjustments to such a complex study. Needless to say, this was a constant source of frustration and anxiety for our team.

Then one day, during a run-of-the-mill check-in with the evaluation manager, they told me, "This is a really difficult thing to say, but we aren't going to continue working with you anymore." Though this happened years ago, my stomach still clenches when I think of that meeting. I was stunned. And terrified, and embarrassed, and really mad.

With the benefit of years' worth of hindsight, it was obvious that our contract wouldn't continue, but at the moment it felt like a huge surprise. Fortunately, our soon-to-be-former client had the good grace to explain, from their perspective, what went wrong.

It turns out that "be flexible" for the client meant that we should have been prepared to completely re-cast the evaluation design in concert with the evaluation manager. The scope of work in our contract was intended only as a placeholder.

Imagine the evaluation manager's surprise and frustration when we tried to hold the line on almost every aspect of that placeholder plan!

Moreover, the evaluation manager was continually receiving requests from their own stakeholders—including elected officials, grantees, and colleagues—to look into different aspects of the programs in our evaluation, potentially requiring shifts to the data we collected. But there were thousands of surveys and dozens of site visits in play for this project, and simply changing course on a dime wasn't feasible for us. To make matters worse, these change requests were also rarely aligned with our data collection schedule. We didn't find a way to balance these tensions.

The evaluation manager, expecting an academically oriented reporting style, also misunderstood our more spacious, findings-first layout as an unprofessional mess rife with formatting errors. It turns out we hadn't communicated our approach very well, and our drafts were therefore perceived as poor-quality deliverables.

And those "internal" grumblings of ours? Our client was keenly aware that we were frustrated by this project.

## LESSONS LEARNED

My lessons learned from this experience apply to me as both a leader and a business owner.

- **If you are frustrated, your client is, too.** This was the huge oversight of mine. I built an internal narrative that set our client as an impossible-to-please person, rather than a partner attempting to get a job done. This led me to assume that we were the only frustrated party, which was utterly incorrect. I missed many valuable opportunities to improve our relationship as a result. Now we encourage our staff to establish and maintain a constructive, growth-oriented tone during internal meetings, even when projects are frustrating or don't go as planned. This positively affects how we interact with our clients, too. There's real power in how you think and talk about clients; as a leader, it is my job to mind the tone we take.

- **Misaligned expectations generate conflict.** We didn't fully understand our client's expectations for the second year of the evaluation, and so we acted in ways that appeared to disregard their needs. On the flip side, they acted as if they paid for a limitless amount of evaluation services by asking for frequent additions to our scope of work, which wasn't true. Unfortunately, we didn't surface these issues in a constructive way, so they festered for everyone. Re-framing this has been helpful to our team, as we're now better able to identify cases where we need to revisit our expectations with our clients.

- **The leader is responsible for addressing conflict.** In part because I wanted to empower the other staff on the project, and mostly because I am deeply conflict averse, I failed to constructively address the problems with this project. The few calls I had with the evaluation manager about our challenges didn't get to root causes, and I spent too much time defending my team instead of understanding the client's perspective. These days I'm much more likely to check in with our clients about how they are feeling about our services, even when they aren't as happy as I'd like. Simply expressing concern about our client's needs goes a long way toward resolving any conflicts that arise.

## REFLECTIVE QUESTIONS

1. What interpersonal skills should a leader on an evaluation team possess in order to successfully identify and address conflict with clients?

2. How might re-framing this evaluation as developmental, rather than summative, have improved everyone's experience?

3. Evaluation can be difficult and frustrating at times. How can evaluators keep a constructive mindset in the midst of challenges?

# THE SCOPE CREEP TRAIN WRECK

## How Responsive Evaluation Can Go Off the Rails

E. Jane Davidson

*E. Jane Davidson, PhD, is an internationally recognized evaluation thought leader, best known for developing evaluation rubrics methodology and for her signature approach of methodologically robust, refreshingly clear, and practical evaluation.*

We all want to be responsive evaluators, for sure. But what happens when there are just far too many things to be responsive to?

This is a story about evaluation scope creep. The hardest thing about scope creep is that it does just that—creeps up on you. It's not until you have made numerous modest adjustments (and inadvertently set the precedent that you are more than willing to make them) that it suddenly dawns on you that it's all gone much too far.

The sum of a long string of perfectly reasonable requests and adjustments can easily end up totaling more than what one evaluation team (let alone a solo evaluator) can cope with. When that happens, it's easy to end up in "train wreck" territory!

How does scope creep happen, how can we see it coming, and what can we do to mitigate the risk? The answers to these questions are what I aim to share with you in this chapter.

## ABOUT ME

I'm Jane Davidson. I've spent the past two decades working as an external evaluator, after spending a few years prior to that doing internal evaluation. Back in 2001, I was hired by the late, great Daniel Stufflebeam to develop, launch, and lead the world's first fully interdisciplinary PhD program in evaluation, at Western Michigan University. Since then I've written a few books on the nuts and bolts of practical evaluation (Davidson, 2005, 2012) and am best known for my work on evaluation rubrics methodology. I've done evaluation work in education, health, philanthropy, transportation, indigenous economic development, social policy, international development, business, and other sectors. These days I focus mostly on building evaluation capacity through coaching, workshops, and online learning opportunities. I also help people build tools and systems for real-time evaluation and evaluative monitoring that can focus, drive, and track change.

This is a story, from very early in my consulting career, of evaluation scope creep due to turbulent shifting contextual sands. Two changes of CEO, a change of government, and multiple organizational restructures led to three changes of internal project manager and numerous shifts in the focus and scope of the evaluation. As I tried to be responsive to all these changes, the project scope and timeline crept more and more, and I ended up way over the deadline and out of budget.

Oh boy, did I learn some lessons from this one!

## DESCRIPTION OF THE EVALUATION

This was a two-year evaluation of a professional development program for federal government employees.

The paying client in this case was a government agency, but there were *many* stakeholders involved. These included multiple agencies who paid to send people on the program, the participants themselves, the organization coordinating the professional development program, and the senior government officials who had approved funding. Plus, of course, the taxpayers who were indirectly bankrolling it all.

The purposes of the evaluation were a combination of formative and summative—to find out how worthwhile the program was as an investment of taxpayer money and people's time and effort, and to identify places where it could be strengthened.

The program was right in my core area of content expertise, and I had a decent timeframe to get the work done—or so I thought. I used a combination of secondary data analysis, document review, direct observation, in-depth interviews, and online surveys to gather the evidence. I used evaluation-specific methodologies, systematic evaluative reasoning, and critical thinking to figure out not just what the program outcomes were but whether they were any good (Davidson, 2005, 2014).

## THE MISTAKE OR CHALLENGE

I took on the evaluation solo, not as part of a team. In hindsight, that was possibly my first mistake. Being early in my career, I felt like I really needed a home run with a decent-sized project that I could say I had done myself and not been "carried" by someone more experienced. I didn't feel I was biting off more than I could chew; in fact, it seemed like the perfect project to provide a solid base of contract work over the next couple of years.

Most importantly, I was actually pretty excited about this evaluation. I had a background in training and development, and my doctorate was in organizational psychology, so I knew what good professional development looked like in a setting like this and how to evaluate its impacts on organizational and system effectiveness. Best of all, I was blessed to be assigned a *wonderful* internal project manager to work with. I remember telling him this was a "dream assignment" for me because it checked so many boxes.

But then all the wheels started to come off. Not in a sudden or catastrophic way, but little by little, and it all added up.

First, the client organization's CEO changed, and the organization was restructured so that the new CEO could put her stamp on a new way of working. I knew that organizational restructures often trigger dysfunctional turnover (that's when high performers leave), so I shouldn't have been as surprised as I was when my awesome project manager (and his manager as well) left and were replaced by people nowhere near as engaged. Waaahh!

My project manager in particular felt *really* bad about leaving me in the lurch by resigning. He went to extraordinary lengths to try and get this project more attention from senior leaders. He spent time bringing the new project manager up to speed and even checked in from his new job to see if I was doing OK.

As if these early upheavals weren't enough to respond to already, it was an election year, and—you guessed it—a new government was elected. Naturally, the priorities for the evaluation changed at that point, to align with the incoming government's priorities. Further staff shuffling ensued, and in came a third project manager who was even more disinterested than the last.

Next—and I was absolutely gobsmacked at this—the CEO changed *yet again*; there was yet another restructure, and I was shunted to a fourth project manager.

Jana Curll

Sorry folks, but I can't let this pass without a total vent about how unbelievably expensive and stressful organizational restructures are, how they are *supposed* to do such amazing things to organizational effectiveness, but they are virtually *never* evaluated! Seriously, can you imagine what a smart move it would be, as a CEO, to hire an evaluation expert to help you think through what you are trying to achieve; whether your proposed organizational restructure is likely to achieve this; what potential negative side effects could potentially ensue; and how you will know early on how well it is all working? Why not be even smarter and get an evaluation team to walk alongside the restructure and give you real-time feedback about the effects as they unfold—and then pull together a synthesis of lessons learned and an overall reflection on whether the whole thing was in fact a good idea at all?

But I digress! Back to my evaluation conundrum . . .

With every change that came hurtling around the corner, there were shifts in focus, which, as a responsive evaluator, I wanted to be sure we addressed appropriately. That meant more time in meetings bringing people up to speed and renegotiating what we were doing and why, which chewed up a lot of days I hadn't budgeted for.

Meanwhile, interest in the evaluation was plummeting because those who had inherited the project had nowhere near the passion of those who originally commissioned it. However, an independent evaluation was a condition to secure ongoing funding for the program, and so (as often happens) the project lived on.

Looking back, I am not sure that there were any red flags that weren't obvious at the time. What I failed to appreciate was the cumulative snowball effect—how a flurry of relatively minor challenges could pile up and leave me feeling overwhelmed and unable to solve them.

Sadly, I can't say that I solved all these problems brilliantly; I just did what was humanly possible at the time.

One thing I did almost instinctively was to build in a lot of real-time updates of my findings, so that key decision makers weren't waiting on one final report but had insights at their fingertips they were able to use immediately to make changes or inform thinking.

In terms of completing the big final report I had agreed to in the contract, this was much more of a challenge. A large chunk of my budgeted time had been plunged into the additional meetings, making changes, and those more useful real-time updates. But with all the changes in personnel, dramatically scaling down the main deliverable would be hard to renegotiate.

I was nervous about ruining my reputation by "flaking" on the final hurdle by not completing the report as agreed. I was equally nervous that if I did flake, the client wouldn't pay the final installment of the contract, which I needed. In the end I decided it was best to just honor the commitment and write a good report, even if it ate up many more hours. I didn't feel I could simply fling together something flimsy based on what I could do quickly, particularly for such a large and multifaceted program. I did have one lovely colleague ask me if I needed help, but by then I was too low on budget to pay for her time, and I certainly didn't want to ask anyone to work on it for free; that wouldn't have felt fair.

So, what happened in the end? Despite the whole thing feeling like a slow motion train wreck from my perspective, the client received useful insights in real time. The write-up of the final report ended up being more an artifact for organizational memory than a new revelation of findings. The report was *very* late in the end, and I felt incredibly embarrassed and disappointed in myself about the timeline blowout. But as I look back now as a more experienced evaluator, it's clear that the real-time reporting I'd done during the project meant that the late final report didn't actually matter that much.

# LESSONS LEARNED

- **Curve balls will come**. The vast majority of the challenges here were well outside of my control. But they are common, and all of us (self-employed or not) can expect curve balls like this at least every couple of years. But even if I had navigated all these challenges like a pro, sometimes evaluation projects are thrown off course because of unforeseen *personal* circumstances. Whether you are an internal or an external evaluator, if you also happen to be a parent, you know all too well that the second you are right down to the wire on a high-stakes project, you are sure to end up with a sick kid home from school needing constant love and attention, who then infects each of the siblings one by one, and then finally the parents get sick. I've been dramatically slowed down on projects over the years with family illnesses, catching the flu or pneumonia myself, sports injuries, tennis elbow, white-knuckle-ride-nausea pregnancies, and all manner of family dramas. Life happens—and when you're self-employed, there is no sick leave allotment to draw on!

- **Prevention, not cure.** The best way to solve a flurry of snowballing problems is to put some safeguards in place that will stop you getting bowled over by them or that will make it possible to navigate your way out more successfully. These days I try to insist on the following for virtually all projects. Many of these ideas translate well for the internal evaluator too, and you will also see some suggestions for those of you who commission and manage evaluations.

  - **Scope creep checkpoints and a contingency budget.** First and perhaps most obviously, I build more frequent review points into every evaluation and discuss with the client having at least a 10% budget contingency for scope creep. I can't always pull this off, but when I'm dealing with experienced clients, they generally see the sense in it. The limiting factor is usually the procurement requirements, which are often far better geared to widget purchasing than a complex and complicated evaluation assignment where not everything is knowable and plannable in advance. I *totally* get the client's need for predictable budgeting, but assigning *all* the risk to me as a sole contractor isn't fair either. If you are one of the internal point people commissioning an evaluation, please do advocate for this contingency budget, for everyone's sake!

  - **Timeline buffers.** Even after 20 years as a self-employed evaluator, I still have to be careful not to assume everything will go smoothly as I map out the contract in my mind's eye and turn that into a budget estimate. There are often very strong "What? It won't take *that* long, will it?" pressures from clients trying to keep the budget down. Internal evaluators can apply this advice to estimating timelines on their own projects, but don't forget you can also help enormously on the commissioning side by influencing your non-evaluator colleagues to think about this. Inserting a few "worst case scenario" buffers into the timeline is realistic and responsible, and clients always appreciate it when I deliver on time despite the inevitable hiccups that occur along the way. Sometimes the buffer isn't needed in the end, and we can all celebrate when I come in under budget and ahead of the timeline.

  - **Shorter Projects "R" Us.** The shorter the project timespan, the less risk there is of scope creep. So, if you can't get a contingency budget, push instead for doing the project in small chunks. I know many people love the security of a long-term project, but for me, a multi-year evaluation signed as a single contract is not so appealing any more. Instead, I like to break it into chunks spanning (ideally) three to six months, maybe 12 months max. The general idea is to set forth and capture the most important insights the client needs right now, then review at or near the completion of that phase and decide what the next chunk of priorities are. In other words, I aim to get a series of smaller contracts rather than one big one. Yes, there is less financial certainty due to the short timelines and there is the option for clients to change their minds, but on the flip side it is much less stressful! More importantly, if things really shift, I'm not locked into an evaluation that the client organization no longer wants.

- **Don't go it alone on a big project.** Contracting solo on a large project is like placing a huge high-stakes bet on yourself and your invincibility. The same is true if you're working as an internal evaluator. Odds are you'll come through and do OK, but there's a serious risk that you won't. The best way to hedge your bets? Collaborate with some trusted colleagues. I know, I know, when you're early in your consulting career it seems counterintuitive to share what few contracts you have with someone else, but even if you involve one other person for 20% of the time, that is one person who could potentially cover for you if anything goes wrong. The added upside is that, if you're like me, working with others helps sweep you along with productivity and motivation. Plus, they will probably want you to give them a hand on something sometime too. Best of all, it makes the work more fun and less isolating. Working as a consultant can feel very lonely at times.

- **Be meticulous about your paper trail.** Work from the assumption that your dream project manager is likely to be replaced at some point during the evaluation. Keep a paper trail detailing any agreements you have made about changes to the scope and focus of the evaluation. Got a client who doesn't "do" email but prefers to talk on the phone or meet face to face instead? Take notes during the call or meeting, tidy them up immediately afterwards, and send a follow-up email summarizing what you agreed. If they like to text you, back up your texts and save them. When the project manager changes, bring that person up to speed with a succinct written summary of changes that have already been agreed to.

- **How do you work best?** This whole scope creep experience highlighted for me that *I am actually a happier evaluator* doing shorter, deep-dive projects than long ones. That was a revelation. For those of us navigating the wonderful rollercoaster ride that is freelance evaluation consulting work, it is crucially important to understand the conditions under which we (as individuals, and/or as teams) work best. It's equally true if you are an internal evaluator. When we can convey that clearly to clients (or managers) and gear our projects to align with those parameters, we end up with much happier clients and employers, as well as much happier selves!

## REFLECTIVE QUESTIONS

1. What safeguards could an evaluator put in place to help minimize the impact of unexpected changes in program context and focus? Include any ideas you thought were worthwhile from this chapter, plus any others you think might be useful.

2.  What could a client organization put in place to help mitigate the kinds of challenges faced by the evaluator? Hint: consider commissioning, contract conditions and milestones, ongoing contract management, and/or internal personnel (project managers, etc.).

3.  Suppose you (as an evaluator or a client) end up partway through a project for which you *hadn't* built in the safeguards, but you start to notice some serious scope creep. What actions could you take midstream to try and mitigate the risks?

# REFERENCES

Davidson, E. J. (2005). *Evaluation methodology basics: The nuts and bolts of sound evaluation*. Thousand Oaks, CA: Sage.

Davidson, E. J. (2012). *Actionable evaluation basics: Getting succinct answers to the most important questions*. Auckland, New Zealand: Real Evaluation.

Davidson, E. J. (2014). Evaluative reasoning. *Methodological Briefs: Impact Evaluation No. 4*. Florence, Italy: UNICEF Office of Research.

# 3

# THE BUFFALO JUMP

## Lessons After the Fall

### Gail Vallance Barrington

*Gail Vallance Barrington, PhD, FCMC, CE, is an award-winning evaluation consultant, writer, and university professor who has led her independent consulting business for over 30 years.*

once coordinated a two-day retreat for an evaluation in a rural area not far from a local geological formation—a buffalo jump.[1] At the end of the first day we laughingly took a team photo lined up along the edge of the same cliff over which indigenous hunters had driven the bison long ago. They were easy prey. Little did I know that, one by one, the project team members and I would eventually disappear ourselves, as if we, too, had fallen over the edge. But I get ahead of myself.

## ABOUT ME

My name is Gail Vallance Barrington. I started my consulting firm, Barrington Research Group, Inc., in 1985 and have conducted over 130 evaluation studies in education, training, health, and research since then. I started as an independent consultant but as my projects grew, so, too, did my staff until I had more than 20 people working with me. When the work started to dry up, I slowly downsized until, today, I am back pretty much where I started, happily working solo. This is one of the many stories I want to share, about how I fell in love with an evaluation, how I made assumptions that blinded me, and how I learned some lessons that remain with me to this day.

## DESCRIPTION OF THE EVALUATION

As I recall it, the project I evaluated related to a health promotion collaboration between the federal government and several provincial health departments, including the one that contracted me. The project focused on community responses to cardiovascular disease (CVD). A steering committee managed the project and was chaired by a university professor. The committee included representatives from a large CVD foundation, the provincial medical association, and the provincial department of health. It was designed as a coalition and was supposed to create bridges between clinical research and health promotion.

The project was managed by a principal investigator (PI) who had received the project grant from the federal government. He was a physician and epidemiologist with a strong background in CVD and a wide circle of international colleagues. His overseas volunteer work and his passion for community development resonated with me and I looked forward to working with him. He was supported by a community-based project coordinator and an evaluation manager who worked for the Department of Health and was responsible for my contract. Because of this rather complex management team, I had no direct access to the steering committee. The grant was housed with the foundation rather than with either the government or the university, a decision made by the PI in order to

---

[1] A buffalo jump is a cliff formation where, as early as 12,000 years ago, Aboriginal hunters herded bison to the edge and drove them over, killing them in mass quantities.

protect the funds from political interference. It seemed clear that his former experience had heightened his awareness of such an eventuality.

The study ran for four years and four demonstration sites were selected. Each had an annual budget that ranged from $65,000 to $85,000. Twenty-five years ago, these were significant resources. The sites were located at health units in different environments around the province and represented urban and rural as well as northern and southern communities. Each site proposed to reduce CVD risk through some combination of activities including exercise, nutrition, changing smoking policies, and conducting health-related research. Their plans varied widely.

- Site 1—holding risk screening clinics, active living events, and stop-smoking activities

- Site 2—developing a sustainable urban health promotion framework through organizational partnerships, capacity building, and needs assessment

- Site 3—creating links with farmers' markets, agricultural groups, and the Women's Institute, and holding risk screening clinics in rural communities

- Site 4—developing and implementing an active living project in two urban elementary/junior high schools

To evaluate these unique initiatives, I selected a case study design, and used a participatory approach, mirroring the project's community development philosophy. We wanted to understand *how* CVD-related information was disseminated and *why* behavior change occurred, if indeed it did. We needed to look for the commonalities, themes, and factors that influenced project development. Unfortunately, our process orientation and interest in health promotion differed from the rigorous, academic perspective held by our federal funder. Early in the evaluation, I knew that their desire for hard data would be strong and so I anticipated significant pressure for concrete evidence and measurable outcomes. The tension between quantitative and qualitative orientations, so prevalent at the time, would play out here as well, so I worked very hard to support my design decisions.

As we began our work, I reviewed a large amount of project documentation, including literature, grant applications, and contract requirements. In all, 511 goals, objectives, questions, strategies, action steps, and indicators had already been developed for the project. Something had to be done!

We spent the next six months developing a global evaluation matrix and fleshing it out with interlocking site-level frameworks that had, as appropriate, shared objectives, evaluation questions, and data collection tools. All the data rolled up to answer the study's overarching questions, but data could also be extracted at the site level. To my mind, it was an elegant and beautiful solution.

We tracked activities, policies, attitudes, and behaviors. We counted partners, volunteers, event attendance, and donations. The wealth of data became overwhelming for the sites to collect and so in Year 2, we began to enter their risk screening data for them although it was not part of our original mandate. I hired an epidemiologist to work with us, and we wove his findings into the case studies. Each quarter, I visited the sites, observed events, and conducted interviews with staff, community partners, volunteers, and participants. It was a busy and complex project with many moving parts and was just the kind of evaluation I liked best. It was also taking more and more of my time.

Each summer the team leaders, site coordinators, and I met for a two-day retreat to discuss and finalize the annual case studies. Then I would prepare a cross-case summary and send the whole package as our annual report to the steering committee. The first retreat was held at a charming country inn. We took a break and visited a local buffalo jump set among the rolling hills. There we took the team photo. Sadly, this early camaraderie was about to fall away. Team members began to disappear. They were reassigned, or removed, or they resigned of their own volition; the reasons for these changes were never very clear to me. Their replacements did not share our understanding about either the project or the evaluation. Not surprisingly, they were keen to ensure their own survival, and an atmosphere of acrimony, suspicion, and fear began to develop.

Simultaneously, the external health environment began to fall apart. The health system was regionalized. The health units we had been working with disappeared, budgets were cut, and staff had to reapply for their former jobs. Education was also in turmoil. School boards were reduced by 70%, and this had a marked effect on teacher morale. The foundation, which had been a key member of the steering committee, underwent a major policy shift and no longer supported health promotion activities. After it withdrew from the committee, the project funds were moved to the university.

The PI saw his control of the project dwindling and when another opportunity presented itself, he resigned and moved across the country. When he left, his position as key researcher was changed to a co-principal investigator (Co-PI) structure and was filled by a senior government administrator and a university physician. Neither was an epidemiologist and neither had strong links to the

CVD community. They favoured a quantitative approach and saw case study research, and this evaluation in particular, as time-consuming, "too broad," and most importantly, too expensive.

Change was rampant. The project coordinator was replaced. Site 1 expanded its project to a second town and doubled its size. Site 2 removed their project manager and the project collapsed. Site 3's key staff member resigned and the project ground to a halt. Site 4 stopped collecting data altogether; its project schools were barely functional—one experienced a complete turnover of its administration, the other's principal was absent for most of the year.

## THE MISTAKE OR CHALLENGE

Remarkably, despite all these changes, I remained flexible and upbeat and was still excited about this complex and challenging evaluation. I tried to foster teamwork and to keep project goals alive, but sometimes it felt as if the evaluation was the only thing that was holding the project together. Although the new management team's rhetoric was positive, their depth of project understanding was limited. Early traction stalled. As Year 4 began, we were in startup mode yet again and the Co-PIs were looking for a quick fix.

When Site 1 expanded, a second site manager was added to manage activities in the new town. Her background in nutritional research had not prepared her for participatory evaluation, and when I circulated the draft Year 3 report prior to the annual retreat, she immediately expressed strong concerns in a letter to the Co-PIs. She suggested that the report was full of inaccuracies and reflected bias on my part. She questioned both my expertise and the evaluation design.

A short time later I got a call from the government Co-PI's office. His secretary asked me rather oddly if I was planning to be in my office the next day. Being very busy getting Year 4 up and running, while dealing with the revisions and finalization of the Year 3 report, I said, "Yes, of course." She suggested that I watch for a courier package and, sure enough, the next day an envelope arrived. It contained a letter terminating my contract as project evaluator and requested that I return all project files to their office within the week.

I was so shocked, I couldn't breathe. I couldn't believe that, so close to completion, and despite all its flaws, this wonderful project was being snatched from me. I, too, had fallen over the edge of the cliff. Why hadn't I seen this failure coming? Where were the fault lines? What false assumptions had I made?

## LESSONS LEARNED

- **A turbulent environment puts an evaluation at risk.** There was so much going on during this period that I believe any evaluation would have been in jeopardy. Government cutbacks reached across all departments. Regionalization and hospital closures put significant stress on the public health system. Facing new roles and reporting requirements, everyone was equally disoriented. When the dust settled, we were looking at a completely new organizational structure. It is likely that the project survived only because of its federal funding and as a by-product, the evaluation tagged along as well. No one was ready to make further changes in these uncertain and shifting times, but the siege mentality did little to bolster support for an innovative approach. Since then, I have viewed any program I am evaluating as a small system embedded in a larger context that must be watched closely. Changes to that external system could have a significant effect on my work, so it is important to imagine and plan for different kinds of project outcomes.

- **Lack of direct access to the steering committee puts the evaluator at a serious disadvantage.** Due to the complex management structure of this project and the fact that I was a contracted evaluator, I had no direct access to the steering committee and remained at arm's length. Information was relayed from the committee to me through several intermediaries, but eventually I received the message that the members felt the evaluation was too broad, too ambitious, and too qualitative, a very different perspective from that of the original PI, who had encouraged me to embrace the evaluation in a collaborative way. I should have insisted on meeting with them directly. I needed to sit down, look them in the eye, and discuss their needs and perspectives. Since this was not possible, I simply buckled down and worked harder to prove the study's worth. However, this turned out to be an unsuccessful strategy.

- **Project staff turnover is a danger sign.** It should have been evident that continual staff turnover represented a serious project flaw and was a danger to the completion of the evaluation. The initial impression of teamwork and collaboration defined my understanding of how the project should function, but even early on, fissures were evident if you knew where to look. For example, the original project coordinator had been a member of the grant-writing team, but she and the PI could not agree on the project vision. Once funding had been obtained, their conflict escalated, and she was soon sidelined. The PI had also not been able to persuade the steering committee to share his vision and so, in retrospect, it's not surprising that he resigned from the very project he had initiated. This should have been a warning sign for me because I had designed the evaluation to reflect his perspective. I no longer had a champion. The constant churn in site players made project cohesion difficult. Ironically, the evaluation seemed healthy and kept expanding, yet the actual project was imploding. Although I can't agree with the way they did it, the new Co-PIs were probably right to cut their losses. Now I view staff turnover as a significant threat to any evaluation and try to work as closely as I can with new staff members. Even so, I still continue to see projects founder for this reason.

- **The value of evaluation is not enough.** Up to the very last day, I believed that the evaluation was strong, appropriate, and valuable. CVD was and continues to be an important health issue. The project supported a good cause and I was hooked. I wanted to know if change was occurring, what it looked like, and what barriers were standing in its way. Traveling to the sites and working with staff was invigorating and fun, and I enjoyed finding solutions to the evaluation challenges as they arose. The fact that these challenges arose with such alarming and increasing frequency did nothing to dampen my enthusiasm. I felt sad and puzzled as team members disappeared over the edge of the cliff, but I never believed my own position was at risk. It was a complete surprise to find myself among the fallen. But my belief in the value of my work was unwarranted. Although much of what occurred was outside of my control, I should have stood back, listened more carefully, and understood how many forces are at play in any single evaluation. I have finally come to understand that it is not the role of an evaluator to solve major program issues or to shore up program staff. If we do, we may be in for a dizzying fall over a cliff ourselves.

# REFLECTIVE QUESTIONS

1. How can the management structure of an evaluation impact its development? What safeguards could the evaluator have implemented in this scenario?

2. The author states that the funder had a rigorous, academic perspective and was likely to press for "hard data." In this context, should the evaluator have made the decision to select a case study methodology? Why or why not?

3. How did the evaluator view the role of the original principal investigator? To what extent did her own attitudes colour her perception of his actions?

# EVALUATOR SELF-EVALUATION

## When Self-Flagellation Is Not Enough

### Emma Williams

*Associate Professor Emma Williams, CE, heads the Evaluation and Knowledge Impact team at the Northern Institute of Charles Darwin University in the Northern Territory of Australia.*

The worst moment came when I realized I had lost the ability to read and write. How can any evaluator, especially a university-based evaluator, work without basic literacy skills? Which skills would go next?

## ABOUT ME

I came to evaluation almost accidentally, which seems to be a traditional route into the field. For some years I was in government, commissioning external evaluations to be used to inform policy and investment frameworks. However, a departmental restructure gave me the chance to go to Charles Darwin University and work on the other side of evaluation, going into the field to collect data, and analyze and present findings. Since then, I have conducted a fair number of evaluations, often in remote locations, and I teach students about aspects of evaluation.

## DESCRIPTION OF THE EVALUATION

In late 2016 I was part of a team conducting a realist evaluation (Westhorp, 2014) that involved document analysis and phone interviews with people from several countries. My role included fieldwork in three African countries and parts of India. Although I received great support from local staff, the work in Africa was particularly challenging. It involved travel in desert and in monsoon conditions, plus working cross-culturally with translators, but I was used to that. What was new was the attitude of the people I was interviewing.

Much of my work is with Australian Aboriginal peoples, who are frank in explaining that they are "the most over-researched people in the world" and who have learned through difficult experience that positive outcomes seldom result from their participation in research and evaluation. In Somaliland, however, I found that many participants were extremely invested in the results of the evaluation. Some participants had travelled long distances just to be included in the interviews, and a number of them expressed extraordinary trust in what their participation in the evaluation would achieve, for example, keep a local program running. I developed an introduction to be delivered by the translator before each interview, setting out that my role was only to present people's voices as accurately as I could and to convey their views to other people who would be making decisions about which programs to fund. I would not be making those decisions. However, as one woman said in tears, people there knew how much it cost to fly someone in. To be worth that amount of investment, I must have considerable influence on the decision making.

I found this view of my role unsettling, and the trust the participants showed in the evaluation process impacted me significantly. However, my discomfort was subsumed in other ongoing urgencies: travelling in sometimes difficult conditions; conducting realist interviews, which needed to be rigorously customized for each participant (Manzano, 2016); and dealing with what was then my greatest fear, technology. I have no technical skills and was often working where there were no places to buy batteries or repair equipment. I was expecting to record about ninety hours of interviews, and there would be no second chances if anything went wrong. Managing the logistics, making sure the equipment worked, and hoping that my back would not go out during off-road travel took up most of my mind that wasn't occupied in updating interview questions. There were often immediate issues to deal with, such as working out how to manage my veils on a windy day after a trip through the mountains to interview an imam, who would be offended by a woman whose hair was showing. In short, it was an evaluation with enough challenges that it was hard for any single issue to stand out, even participant trust.

I arrived home in early December with what turned out to be well over a thousand pages of transcripts to analyze. The client wanted a draft report by the end of the month and although I was only the second author, I had a lot to do to make it happen. I also had multiple other commitments, including an interstate evaluation trip I had committed to before we won the international contract and a move for our entire household across the continent, scheduled for 27 December. I spent most of Christmas Day analyzing data and packing. January was even busier than December, and February was almost as busy.

# THE MISTAKE OR CHALLENGE

Although I had been given a few introductions to people in our new home city of Perth, I wanted to make sure I met all my work commitments before settling in. I didn't feel I could take time off for leisure, even on weekends, until I was caught up. In addition, there were new work projects commencing.

I was finding it oddly difficult to concentrate, so I resolved to try harder. It was frustrating; although I was pushing myself harder and harder, it seemed that I was producing less and less. I had felt overloaded several times before in my career and had worked my way through those moments successfully, but something about this situation felt different. I was hearing a continuous refrain in my head: "I can't give them what they need." It was as annoying as a buzzing mosquito. It was also puzzling. Who did "them" refer to? I didn't pursue that question and instead worked on ignoring the refrain as I wrote up reports.

The lowest point came one day when I went to my desk to work and realized that I could not read. I could identify individual words, but a sentence was hard to process and a paragraph made no sense at all. I tested myself on a page of Jane Austen. Reading evaluation texts was one thing, but if I could not make sense of Jane, whose books I had read and re-read so often that I could recite passages by heart, the situation was serious. It was. I could not make out what any of the characters were doing. Who was this fellow Darcy?

Unable to read or write, I began to wonder what might be next to go. Would I forget how to walk next? I resolved to be very careful going downstairs.

Jana Curll

One helpful development came the next day when my back, which had survived all the off-road travel, went into spasm when I intervened in a dogfight near our new rental. The doctor prescribed some pills that effectively turned off my brain for a few days, which I spent in bed staring at the ceiling. Once I could walk again, however, I returned to my previous strategy of just trying to work harder. At this point, I could only read and retain a few paragraphs at a time, so I developed ways to work around this (not so) minor inconvenience. My techniques, although they showed a certain imagination, could be summed up as variants of mental self-flagellation. I convinced myself that I simply needed to apply myself harder. In particular, I beat myself up about thinking I had problems when there were other people in the world with *real* problems.

Identifying the genuine problem, and finding a more effective way to tackle it as an evaluator, took an embarrassingly long time. My devotion to duty, stubbornness, and stamina enabled me to persist with exactly the wrong strategy for months. It was not until I returned to the east coast for conference and work commitments that colleagues observed me with some concern, gently sat me down, and began to untangle some of my thinking. One colleague with a background in disaster recovery helped me to understand how the responsibility I felt for the evaluation participants who had put their trust in me was driving the "I can't give them what they need" refrain in my head. Another colleague spent a good deal of time showing me how my long-established approach of "Just work harder" was counterproductive in this situation. It was not only achieving diminishing returns but also getting in the way of identifying the real issues. An ounce of self-care, she tried to convince me, could lead to a pound of improved productivity. If I was concerned about the trust evaluation participants placed in me, taking more time for myself would enable me to better meet their needs as well.

With the support of these colleagues, I was able to initiate a genuine self-evaluation and identify more effective approaches to my work situation. I was fortunate to have these particular colleagues, as well as supportive clients and employer. Once I was able to articulate my situation, support was offered and deadlines adjusted. I found it difficult, though. I still feel chagrined that clients did not get the products in a timely fashion and am sorry for the extra load I put on some of my co-authors. I continued to have anxious moments for a few months whenever I submitted anything in writing or spoke to audiences for fear I would lose my language capacity again and begin to speak in gibberish. I kept an eye on the audiences to make sure they were not looking confused or horrified, which would tip me off that something was wrong. Fortunately, it appeared on each occasion that I was making sense, or at least speaking in English.

Some of the longer term effects of my experience have provided unexpected benefits. To better honor the voices of participants who put so much trust in the evaluation process, we are initiating a new style of report that enables their views to be presented more comprehensively to decision makers. My colleagues and I are improving our contingency planning and building up the number of people to whom evaluation tasks can be delegated. Work is also underway to develop prebriefing and debriefing guidelines for evaluators heading into conflict and trauma situations. Although there are ethics guidelines to protect participants in these situations, there is nothing currently that addresses the evaluator's own needs.

Although these changes are important, it seems to me that there is an even more fundamental issue that was revealed by my struggles, that is, the critical importance of evaluator self-evaluation.

To obtain the Canadian Evaluation Society's (CES) Credentialed Evaluator designation, which I achieved earlier in 2016, I had to write dozens of paragraphs on various evaluation competencies, as defined by the CES. One of them was:

*1.6 Aware of self as an evaluator (knowledge, skills, dispositions) and reflects on personal evaluation practice (competencies and areas for growth).*

In my paragraphs, I noted occasions when I had identified gaps in my evaluation knowledge and skills and had found resources to balance the areas where I was weak. These reflections were accurate, but limited, as they reflected only my technical evaluation skills. What I did not reflect on, but what turned out to be critical in this case, were the qualities I have as a person and the impact of those qualities on my evaluation practice.

I typically have more energy than I know what to do with, and I usually enjoy the stimulation that arises from being engaged in multiple projects. In the situation described in this chapter, however, I allowed my workload to get out of hand, and the resulting physical tiredness made it easy to lose perspective on how to be sustainably productive. That lack of perspective led to guilt and an unhelpful dynamic that made me less effective even as I drove myself to work ever harder.

In the end, the solutions for my problem came from my interactions with evaluation colleagues. The relationships I have nurtured over the years ended up helping me to see what I could not see for myself and enabled me to genuinely reflect and self-evaluate. The paragraph I wrote for the CES competency ended with a statement I would now even more strongly endorse: "*I have also cultivated a network of expert colleagues who (amongst more important functions) help me identify where I need further development, and are not backward with frank advice.*"

# LESSONS LEARNED

- **Evaluation involves the whole person.** In thinking about one's strengths and weaknesses as an evaluator, considering technical skills is not enough. Personal qualities such as interpersonal skills (with fellow evaluators, not just clients and evaluation participants), conscientiousness, and self-care skills can play as large a role as the ability to develop theories of change or the ability to analyze data.

- **Self-evaluation is vital.** If you are struggling to evaluate yourself effectively, it may be time to take a break from evaluating others. Most of us, even with a reasonable degree of self-awareness, have one or more blind spots. In these cases, seek the input of others whose judgment you trust and whose perspectives can complement your own.

- **Self-care is vital.** Evaluations can be stressful, especially if program participants have high trust and expectations, or when they involve "speaking truth to power." It is easy to lose perspective when one is overtired or overloaded with tasks. Similar to the oxygen mask rule in planes, where passengers are directed to don their own mask first before helping others, evaluation stakeholders, both commissioners and participants, are likely to be better served by an evaluator who is in good physical and emotional health.

# REFLECTIVE QUESTIONS

1. What are your own strengths and weaknesses as an evaluator, including your personal qualities?

2. What are some self-care strategies you could use?

3. What other resources could you cultivate to support your strengths and balance your weaknesses as an evaluator?

# REFERENCES

Manzano, A. (2016). The craft of interviewing in realist evaluation. *Evaluation*, *22*(3), 342–360.

Westhorp, G. (2014, September). *Realist impact evaluation: An introduction* (Overseas Development Institute Working and Discussion Paper). Retrieved from https://www.odi.org/publications/8716-realist-impact-evaluation-introduction

# 5

# THAT ALIEN FEELING

## Engaging All Stakeholders in the Universe

Richard Brown

## Hallie Preskill

*Hallie Preskill, PhD, is a managing director at FSG, where she leads the firm's Strategic Learning and Evaluation practice.*

As I listened to one of the evaluation stakeholders yelling at me over the phone, I wondered why he was so furious with me. Unfortunately, my response to him got me into deeper trouble. I'd like to share a story about a time early in my career, when I failed to engage a key group of stakeholders in an evaluation, and the profound impact it has had on my evaluation thinking and practice ever since then.

## ABOUT ME

I fell in love with evaluation in 1979, two classes into my first evaluation course. After doing a year-long evaluation internship and getting my PhD from the University of Illinois at Urbana-Champaign in 1984 (in training and organizational development and evaluation), I have spent the last 34 years as a professional evaluator, engaged in teaching, researching, and writing about evaluation, and conducting evaluations as an external evaluator in multiple sectors. For the last nine years, I have had the privilege of overseeing FSG's Strategic Learning and Evaluation practice, where we work primarily with foundations, non-profits, corporate philanthropy, and government agencies. I was also proud to serve as president of the American Evaluation Association (AEA) in 2007 and spent a total of six years on AEA's board of directors.

## DESCRIPTION OF THE EVALUATION

From 1989 to 1991 I was the evaluator of the Saturn School for Tomorrow in St. Paul, Minnesota (grades 4–8). The school was an inspiration for the New American Schools Development Corporation competition and initiative in 1992, which was announced by former president George H. W. Bush when he visited the Saturn School in 1991. Among many things, the school emphasized individual student growth plans, one computer for every two students, and a curriculum that changed every six to eight weeks depending on students' interests and needs. The school was considered to be a transformational experiment, and it received various state waivers to allow it to be groundbreaking. It also received national attention and was written up in *Time* and *Newsweek* magazines.

As an external, formative evaluator, I had negotiated my role as one who would provide feedback to the teaching staff and write a report at the end of each school year. To address the 35 key evaluation questions over the three years, I spent about eight hours a week on site, during which time I interviewed teachers, staff, administrators, and students; conducted observations and document reviews; took over 400 photographs; and collected and analyzed test score data. The school was governed loosely by a principal and four "lead" teachers. There was also a parent council that was involved in limited ways. As part of my data collection efforts, I conducted focus groups with parents and administered a mailed survey to all parents.

In the evaluation plan, I noted the following as stakeholders in the three-year evaluation:

- Teachers and administrators (Primary audience)

- Parents of students (Secondary audience)

- District administrators and the public (Tertiary audience)

I envisioned the evaluation as responsive and stakeholder focused. As always, my goal was to provide useful information to the various audiences that would help them understand the school's efforts and impact on students, and to make formative improvements along the way. For each of the three years, I collected data from September through June, and then spent my summers analyzing the data and writing up a 50-page year-end report with an executive summary that was delivered in late August, just prior to the new school year beginning.

## THE MISTAKE OR CHALLENGE

As with any innovation, there are things that work well and things that don't work so well. Not surprisingly, the evaluation of the Saturn School surfaced many challenges and issues in its first two years. I noted the following in the Year 2 report:

> "While the report cites numerous examples of successes experienced by students, staff, and parents, it also discussed some serious issues which tend to cast a negative light on certain aspects of the school. Again, these findings are part of the process, and in no way reflect an end to this process. In fact, early indications are that many of the problems Saturn faced in the second year, are being resolved in its third year."

This evaluation report was delivered to the teachers and administrators, as usual, in August, but was released to the parents a few weeks later. It was not my common practice at the time to share it with the secondary audiences for their review and feedback before finalizing the report. More on this later.

Somewhere between September and November, the report was shared with the school's Parent Council. One day, I received a call from the head of the council, where he proceeded to yell at me for failing to tell the full story of the school. He angrily explained that he was speaking on behalf of the other parents and wondered why I did not present more of the positive outcomes and successes of the school in the report. Even though I reminded him that I had interviewed many people, including parents, he accused me of not sufficiently including the parents' perspectives. He further informed me that he had conducted a telephone survey of Saturn parents and their most common response was, "Thank God for Saturn. My child was failing at the other schools he went to. At Saturn, he is doing very well and enjoys it." He also said that he knew that many of the issues in the report were already being addressed. In sum, he felt that the evaluation report as written was (a) too negative—it didn't balance the issues with the successes, and (b) outdated by the time it was written. He also wondered why the Parent Council didn't get a preview copy before it was finalized. As I listened to him, I felt like an alien from outer space—why was he saying this? What didn't he understand? Why was he so furious? I found his accusations totally disorienting.

My response got me into further trouble. I explained that the primary audience was the teaching staff and school administrators. Though I immediately regretted my next statement, it was something I could not unsay. Although I don't remember my exact words, it was something to the effect that parents, as the secondary audience, were not as important as the primary audience, since it is the teachers and administrators who would need to make any improvements to the school experience. This did not go over well, and he demanded to know what I would do to make sure that the world knew enough about the school's accomplishments. I decided that the best and perhaps only approach was to invite the Parent Council to write a rejoinder or amendment to the report (which had not yet been released to the public). He agreed to do this, and it became an appendix to the report. In it, he wrote:

Jana Curll

"While we share many of the concerns the report raises and agree that many topics raised by the report need further assessment, we take satisfaction in the progress Saturn has made. . . . We continue to believe that with hard work by the staff and continued participation by parents, Saturn can become a shining star in the successful St. Paul Magnet program and a guide to the evolution of education in all St. Paul Schools."

He also listed eight successes and four areas where improvements were already being made. Even though I had incorporated parents' perspectives into the overall set of findings and recommendations, the Parent Council felt it was important to state their views in this format.

For the third and several years thereafter, the school continued to experience challenges that surfaced in its early days of its implementation. In spite of various efforts, the school converted back to operating as a regular school in 2003.

Evaluating the Saturn School was an incredibly rich learning experience. It helped me experiment with and hone my data collection and analysis skills. It provided me an opportunity to study an educational transformation initiative up close over a protracted period of time. It laid the foundation of my interest in developmental evaluation, and it provided a hard-earned lesson in stakeholder engagement. As we all know, it's so much easier to see certain things in hindsight, and this experience was no exception.

## LESSONS LEARNED

The final formal outcome of this story is the letter written by the head of the Parent Council. However, the informal outcomes of this experience were more about when and how to involve various stakeholders in an evaluation process. These include the following:

- **Be thoughtful about the language you use.** Whereas many don't distinguish between the terms "audience" and "stakeholder," I believe there is a difference and have amended my language to accommodate this. Instead of using the term "audience," I now prefer to talk about "stakeholders." This change reflects my belief in the critical importance of evaluation use and the assumption that the word "stakeholders" implies intended users. The word "audiences" connotes a more passive recipient of information. I think part of my problem was I thought of the teachers as stakeholders and the parents as audiences. This likely muddied how I thought about stakeholder engagement.

- **Develop a stakeholder engagement plan.** This experience deepened my learning about the importance of developing a stakeholder engagement plan. At the beginning of an evaluation, I now consider the various stakeholders and how they might wish to be engaged in the evaluation's design and review of preliminary findings and any reports. Of course, this involves when, where, and how their engagement is appropriate and ethical. I also don't refer to them as primary, secondary, or tertiary anymore either!

- **Hold data interpretation meetings.** For the third and final year, I made sure to vet my findings with the Parent Council so I could more effectively incorporate their feedback and perspectives. Nowadays, I routinely facilitate data interpretation meetings, where I share analyzed quantitative and/or qualitative data with stakeholders to collaboratively develop interpretations, judgments, and recommendations. This not only helps people understand the data, but it builds their capacity to think evaluatively and to appreciate the value of professional evaluation practice.

# REFLECTIVE QUESTIONS

1. What might have been different with this scenario if the concept and practice of developmental evaluation was known at the time? How, if at all, would the stakeholders have been involved in a different way?

2. The evaluator's approach to resolving the issue with the Parent Council was to invite them to write a rejoinder or addendum to the evaluation report. What other options might she have considered for them to contribute after the report had been written?

3. What are some other ways to engage stakeholders in an evaluation process, so that their involvement adds value and meets their engagement needs?

# 6

# SEEDS OF FAILURE

## How the Evaluation of a West African Agricultural Scale Up Project Went Awry

Virginia Tech

### Thomas Archibald

*Thomas Archibald, PhD, is an assistant professor and extension specialist in Virginia Tech's Department of Agricultural, Leadership, and Community Education, where his research and practice focus primarily on evaluation capacity building and evaluative thinking in community development contexts.*

There I was, sitting in a workshop in Togo with 13 exasperated monitoring and evaluation (M&E) specialists from 13 different West African countries, translating a 20-page survey from English to French that focused on minute agronomic details such as the dry matter and water content of corn in different research plots. I began to wonder how—more than one year into a three-year project—we would even get our baseline data collected.

## ABOUT ME

I am Thomas Archibald, an assistant professor in the Department of Agricultural, Leadership, and Community Education at Virginia Tech. I have worked on and evaluated diverse agricultural and community development projects across West Africa and elsewhere. In the past few years, in international development and other contexts, there has been a growing recognition of the importance of complexity-aware approaches to monitoring and evaluation. I would like to share a story of what *not* to do when faced with evaluating a complex agricultural development initiative.

## DESCRIPTION OF THE EVALUATION

Some years ago, I worked on a contract to evaluate a project that was supposed to scale up an improved way of growing maize (corn). The approach used few external inputs (like water, fertilizers, pesticides, and other products), relying instead on a handful of simple management techniques about how to plant and tend to the maize seedlings. As such, the approach had the potential to greatly increase yields for resource-poor farmers with small plots of land, helping them enhance both their families' nutrition and their financial situation. The three-year project was funded by a major international funding agency, and the implementation was led by a U.S. university where the maize-growing approach had been refined, in partnership with an African center of excellence on maize.

One source of complexity of the project was its intention to scale up the approach to 13 West African countries, some Francophone and others Anglophone, and all characterized by their own rich diversity of geography, culture, ecosystems, political systems, and more. To scale up the approach, the project used workshops, peer-to-peer learning, demonstration plots, media campaigns, and more. On the ground, the project was to be implemented via a network of national agricultural research and development institutions (Centers of Agricultural Productivity, or CAPs) that were also funded by the major international agency funding the maize project. I was the lead evaluation coordinator, based in the United States as a consultant. I worked with another regional evaluation specialist based in West Africa with the network of CAPs with whom I would eventually work (hereafter "the regional M&E specialist"). Each of the 13 countries represented in the network also had a national M&E specialist, who would be called on to implement the project's M&E plan at the national level.

# THE MISTAKE OR CHALLENGE

We failed terribly on many fronts. The seeds for our failure were planted well before the project was even underway. I helped write the proposal, sitting in the basement of the agricultural library at the U.S. university, with a university maize researcher (hereafter "the researcher") and the coordinator of a regional African center of excellence on maize ("the coordinator"). Over a period of a few days while the coordinator was visiting the university, we wrote both the project design and the M&E plan, complete with indicators and targets. Project implementation in each country fell largely to the experts working at the national CAPs, and the centrally funded project was led by the researcher and the coordinator providing system-level coordination and leadership. The M&E system was supposed to be implemented by the national M&E specialists based at the 13 national CAPs around West Africa. However, without much knowledge of the CAP system, I was embedding into the project proposal an evaluation approach that would only later be shared with the people responsible for implementing it. That was mistake number one.

I identified three needs for the evaluation, each adding an additional layer of complexity:

- Integrate multiple levels of the system: local, national, and regional.

- Integrate diverse agronomic and social indicators.

- Involve standardization for regional aggregation of data, yet also localization to deal with the realities of diverse contexts.

Based on the desired outcomes of the project, I articulated a series of indicators and drafted surveys, tracking forms, and other data collection tools and approaches that I believed would gather credible evidence on the outcomes of interest. I also designed an M&E system (i.e., documents providing guidance, plus web-based systems for communications and data management) that would provide a mechanism to manage roles and responsibilities and ensure that data could flow up and provide aggregated regional results. Because it was early in my career as an evaluator, this was one of the most comprehensive evaluation systems I'd put together, and although I knew it had room for improvement, I was pretty proud of it. Unfortunately, this institutional and administrative arrangement for M&E would become a major cause of the dysfunction moving forward.

Once the project was funded, the first activity was a workshop with the national CAP staff, held in Senegal. The 13 CAP M&E specialists got together, with the regional M&E specialist and I leading a session to review and validate the M&E plan, including the logical framework and some of the key indicators and assumptions. Boy, was I glad to meet the regional M&E specialist at that validation workshop in Senegal! She had a deep understanding of the CAP system and of the practical ins and outs of agricultural development M&E in the region more generally. If she had been involved in the evaluation design, we probably could have avoided many of our mistakes. A few months later, we held a second workshop in Togo for CAP M&E personnel, which coincided with an already scheduled regional meeting of key CAP actors, to go over the data collection tools (in French and English) and to validate the design in terms of content, understandability, and feasibility.

By the time of this second workshop in Togo, the seeds of our failure had germinated and were growing into strong seedlings of disaster. They were fertilized by the administrative inertia that sometimes impedes the timely launching of research and development projects, regardless of the funder. New accounts need to be established, paperwork needs to be signed, and funding often needs to flow through numerous administrative units before it is ready to be spent. We were almost through Year One (of three) by the time we were meeting in Togo to validate the M&E data collection tools, and the baseline data were still far from being collected.[1] We knew we needed to get moving, but we also thought we'd be OK. We weren't.

In hindsight, there were two major axes of failure in this evaluation, one which we saw coming, the other which was more of a surprise as it happened. The first, as mentioned previously, was that the national CAP M&E specialists who were expected to do the on-the-ground evaluation in each country had not been adequately included in the evaluation planning. They received slow and mixed messages about what they were expected to do, and they weren't able to integrate the M&E activities of this project into their ongoing annual planning and budgeting. The project entrusted the M&E activities to CAP staff who were already fully occupied in the M&E of other projects in their country that were higher priorities for them. In essence, the data collection was like an unfunded mandate for them, and one that arrived too late for them to practically address given their workflow management constraints. I must admit this wasn't exactly a surprise, as I did have a sense this would happen, even during the proposal-writing stage. The researcher and I specifically asked if it would be a problem to rely on the national CAP M&E experts without funding them or involving them in the planning process, but the coordinator, who knew the CAP system well, said, "No, it's their job; they will do it." In practice, it turned out that neither the researcher nor the coordinator had any control over the M&E specialists' workflow. And neither did we.

The second more unanticipated challenge was that the researcher (who had hired me as a consultant) consistently requested round after round of changes to the evaluation plan and data collection tools. In particular, he wanted to turn two surveys that were aimed at gathering data on farmers' maize yields and income indicators into exceedingly detailed and complicated maize research data

---

[1] Michael Bamberger, Jim Rugh, and Linda Mabry have made an art form of dealing with this all-too-common problem in international development evaluation, described in their RealWorld evaluation approach (Bamberger, Rugh, & Mabry, 2011).

collection tools, collecting way more information than was needed to respond to the key evaluation questions and effectively rendering the tools infeasible to use. Exacerbating this challenge was an existing friendship and work relationship between the researcher and me, both of which complicated the power dynamics and the interactive nature of the problem, as Jean King and Laurie Stevahn (2012) discuss in their book *Interactive Evaluation Practice: Mastering the Interpersonal Dynamics of Program Evaluation*. I felt really conflicted, frustrated, confused, and unsure of how to proceed.

Jana Curll

Both of these challenges came to a head at the Togo workshop. The national CAP M&E specialists rightly complained that it was too late to insert the required data collection tasks into their annual work plans and budgets, so the baseline would be delayed another year. As a systems issue, some also felt unsure as to why they were there, since their supervisors had not explained the modus operandi of the project to them very well. Tensions were high, and one participant was effectively staging a silent sit-in. Yet even those national CAP M&E specialists who wanted to be there and wanted the evaluation to succeed were justifiably concerned that the tools designed to collect data on maize yield and income were not appropriate for the evaluation and would not be remotely feasible to use. This was where we inadequately addressed the integration, within the M&E system, of diverse agronomic and social indicators. Unfortunately, we had little recourse at this point, as these two tools had already been developed (and serially revised) by the researcher, who was the project lead. Basically, we were left to commiserate with the exasperated national CAP M&E specialists. Even after the Togo fiasco, the researcher requested additional iterations of the data collection tools. He also seemed to have a different understanding of "baseline" than I did. For me (and the regional and national M&E specialists as well), the baseline would have been the first application of all of our data collection tools, but for the researcher, with his background in maize research, the baseline was supposed to be a larger study of the current practice of maize growing in the 13-country region. These separate understandings of the baseline's purpose further clouded and delayed the implementation of the study.

In the end, I needed to leave the project because of an unrelated change in my employment status (my university named me Chief of Party of a U.S. Agency for International Development project, a role in which outside consulting was prohibited), which gave me an opportunity to rather gleefully pass the project onto another evaluation firm (with due warning). Through the grapevine, I heard that the other firm did what it could, given the circumstances, and the project came to an end after its three years of funding was up. There was only a meagre harvest of M&E results, but a bumper crop of lessons learned for me as a young evaluator.

## LESSONS LEARNED

- **Listen to your gut and communicate your concerns from the outset.** Even the researcher expressed concerns during the proposal-writing phase about the unfunded mandate of data collection for the national CAP M&E specialists. He and I were worried this could scuttle the evaluation, and we were right. We should have addressed those concerns head on by building in a budget and a timeline that included these important actors in our planning. It's important to engage key stakeholders in the evaluation, especially those who are critical to its successful implementation.

- **Be clear about the purpose of an evaluation and the distinction between evaluation and research.** A common question for novice evaluators, and a perennial topic of conversation on evaluation list serves, is the difference between research and evaluation. In this failure case, we should have been stricter about keeping the data collection tools pegged to the evaluation questions, indicators, and purpose of the evaluation, and not let the researcher invade our process with "We need to know" and "Wouldn't it be nice to know" input, which led to the creation of long, unwieldy, and infeasible data collection tools.

- **Put in place the right institutional arrangements.** It is important to clearly provide not only sufficient funding for M&E activities but also the necessary institutional and administrative structures. Roles, responsibilities, reporting channels, organizational hierarchies, loci of control and power, timeline planning, and task prioritization must be explicitly addressed by key stakeholders to avoid M&E failure.

- **Be present to interpersonal factors.** Were you hired by a friend or close colleague? Are you part of an evaluation with "interesting" power relations? Be careful how those interpersonal factors may affect the evaluation. It is difficult yet essential, regardless of the power dynamics and relationships you have with the client (who is also signing your paycheck), that you remain able to deliver hard news in clear and firm ways when necessary—even if it means jeopardizing new contracts or old friendships.

# REFLECTIVE QUESTIONS

1. If a friend or close acquaintance offers you a contract, would you take it? If so, what management strategies would you put in place to handle any interpersonal issues that may arise?

2. What evaluation planning processes could you adopt to ensure that the "on-the-ground" needs of data collectors are adequately taken into consideration ahead of time?

3. How would you personally distinguish between research and evaluation? If there is an opportunity to collect interesting research data related to your evaluand, but which is not connected to your evaluation questions, should you do so? Why or why not?

# REFERENCES

Bamberger, M., Rugh, J., & Mabry, L. (2011). *RealWorld evaluation: Working under budget, time, data, and political constraints* (2nd ed.). Thousand Oaks, CA: Sage.

King, J. A., & Stevahn, L. (2012). *Interactive evaluation practice: Mastering the interpersonal dynamics of program evaluation*. Thousand Oaks, CA: Sage.

# 7

# I DIDN'T KNOW
# I WOULD BE A TIGHTROPE
# WALKER SOMEDAY

## Balancing Evaluator
## Responsiveness and Independence

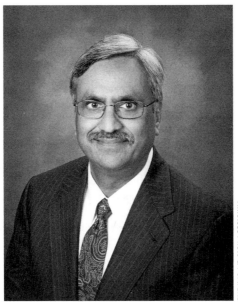

Timeless Photo & Portraits

### Rakesh Mohan

*Rakesh Mohan is the director of the Office of Performance Evaluations, an independent and nonpartisan agency of the Idaho State Legislature.*

N ewspaper headlines such as "Legislature's Auditor Defends Teacher Report" (Popkey, 2013) are not new to me. They are part and parcel of being an evaluator or auditor in a public policy environment. However, when I am one of the subjects of these headlines, they force me to think whether I could have done something different to avoid being the center of media attention.

## ABOUT ME

My name is Rakesh Mohan, and I am a tightrope walker. I regularly balance the tension between independence and responsiveness because I work as an evaluator in a public policy environment. In 2002, I was appointed as the director of the Office of Performance Evaluations (OPE), an independent and nonpartisan agency of the Idaho Legislature. I am only its second director since the office was statutorily created in 1994.

## DESCRIPTION OF THE EVALUATION

Before I relate my story, let me first describe for you the environment in which I work. OPE's mission is to promote confidence and accountability in state government through independent assessment of state programs and policies. The Joint Legislative Oversight Committee (JLOC) is an eight-member bipartisan committee that selects evaluation projects for us to work on. In an overwhelmingly Republican state, JLOC is the only legislative standing committee that is equally bipartisan and is co-chaired by a Republican and a Democrat legislator. The committee is also equally divided between the two chambers of the legislature.

The selection of evaluation projects takes place at a public meeting of JLOC. The members of JLOC decide which evaluation projects we will work on from a list of evaluation requests that are submitted by members of the legislature. These requests vary in their specificity—some are very brief and only ask us to evaluate a program or policy, some give details about specific concerns legislators have about a program, whereas others request answers to specific evaluation questions. Once projects are assigned to us, we determine the evaluation scope with input from JLOC members and relevant stakeholders. We then independently decide the evaluation approach and methodology, conduct the evaluation, and develop findings, conclusions, and recommendations. Our work is guided by recognized evaluation and government auditing standards.

We release our evaluation reports at public meetings of JLOC. The findings, conclusions, and recommendations in our reports are not intended to reflect the views of JLOC or its individual members. Prior to a report's release, JLOC members and a handful of other relevant members of the legislative leadership are provided with the final report in advance of the meeting. They, however, do not have any role in modifying the report's findings, conclusions, or recommendations.

Both the governor and the agency or program that we evaluate are given an opportunity to provide their written responses to our draft report, and these responses are included in the final report.

## THE MISTAKE OR CHALLENGE

This section describes three challenges I experienced in 2008, 2013, and 2014. All three had a common theme: they reflected the inherent tension that exists when conducting evaluations in a high-stakes public policy environment. The tension for evaluators lies between being responsive to evaluation sponsors and stakeholders while at the same time maintaining independence from these very same people. Being responsive means meeting their information needs, that is, fully answering their questions, offering practical recommendations or options, and respecting their time constraints. This requires listening to their issues and concerns and understanding the evaluation context. Maintaining independence, on the other hand, means guarding the entire evaluation (scope, approach and methodology, findings, conclusions, and recommendations) from their undue influences. For example, sometimes evaluation sponsors want to use the office to deliver a message that they support as part of their political agendas. These two seemingly conflicting demands on government evaluators like myself create a natural tension that can appear in many ways and during any stage of an evaluation. Despite the useful guidance and safeguards offered by evaluation and auditing standards, managing this type of tension feels like walking a tightrope at times.

My first challenge came in 2008 at a public JLOC meeting where my ability to walk the tightrope was tested. JLOC members discussed and voted on a proposed rule relating to evaluation scope (Idaho Legislature, 2008). The proposed rule said that my office, the OPE, would draft an evaluation scope and provide it to JLOC members for input, but OPE would have the final say. Up until this time, committee rules had not been clear on who had the final say in deciding the scope of an evaluation. I explained to the committee that the scoping process is very close to determining the evaluation approach and methodology, and any biases injected into this process would likely affect the outcome of the evaluation. Therefore, to ensure the scope was free from political influences, or even the appearance of such, OPE needed to have the final say.

Several JLOC members were uncomfortable with this proposed rule. They mentioned several good reasons why they wanted the committee to have the final say. For example, one member asked, "What recourse would the committee have if a scope headed in the wrong direction?" Another wanted "room for negotiation if the scope needed tweaking to gain committee consensus." Although I had expected some disagreement to the proposed rule, I had not quite prepared myself to publicly respond to that disagreement. Two thoughts raced quickly through my head: (1) acquiesce to their concerns to avoid disagreeing with them in public, or (2) defend my position even at the risk of publicly disagreeing with my high-profile bosses. Obviously, it is not prudent to have conflicts or tension with one's employer. It creates an unpleasant work environment, compromises organizational effectiveness, erodes professional credibility, provides fodder for rumors and unpleasant stories in the media, and increases the likelihood of getting fired. And yes, sometimes the conflict is unavoidable and one is left with defending his or her position.

I felt my tightrope begin to wobble. I tried to assure the committee that I would do everything to ensure the evaluation scope was responsive to their information needs by seeking input from them and other legislators. Supporting my position, one committee member said, "[Giving] JLOC approval of scopes was like a home inspection with restrictions; an expert hired to inspect a house is told not to look in the crawl space, closets, or attic. Because the inspection is manipulated, the likely outcome would not be a true picture of the condition of the house." She further said she "appreciated the explicit wording in the rule to discuss the scope with members and seek input, but going beyond discussion invited trouble." Another committee member said, "Select the topic, hand the project over to OPE, and get out of the way—it's the safest and most professional way." After a long and tense discussion, the rule was approved as I had proposed. Even though I got my way that day, I was totally shaken up from the experience. Upon reflection, I believe I could have done a better job of privately explaining to JLOC members the importance of protecting the scoping process from political influences—but I should have done so prior to the day of the public committee vote. Also, I should have had this conversation with each committee member individually. This is because of two reasons: (1) many people, and public officials in particular, do not like to be put in an uncomfortable position publicly, and (2) individual conversations would have likely resolved any misunderstanding between us and fostered greater trust.

My second challenge occurred in 2013 when we released an evaluation report on workforce issues affecting public school teachers. The following day, the *Idaho Statesman*, Idaho's major newspaper, referenced the report with this front-page headline: "Survey Shows Teachers' Worries" (Dvorak, 2013). The headline, I believe, unfortunately added fuel to some of the highly contentious public education issues that had been in the news for several years. Consequently, our evaluation was not well received by certain members of the legislature, particularly the chairs of the Senate and House Education Committees. They questioned our evaluation methodology and conclusions. This was worrisome to me because the chair of the Senate Education Committee was the one who had originally requested the study.

After the report release, both privately and publicly, I defended our report and respectfully explained to both committee chairs the reasons behind our conclusions in the report. Their biggest concern was the qualitative nature of our survey methodology, preferring evidence derived from quantitative analysis. To them, numbers constituted "real" data and qualitative information was nothing more than anecdotes and opinions. At times our conversation felt like we were speaking two different languages. We had different views of data, evidence, and evaluation methodologies.

About a month later, one of these private meetings ended up *again* on the front page of the *Idaho Statesman*; however, this time it was to note that "the survey that found 'despair' among Idaho's educators caused a flap,

Jana Curll

but top lawmakers say they support the examiners" (Popkey, 2013). In our defense, the Speaker of the House was reported as saying, "Performance audits are a tricky business. You're calling balls and strikes." It was comforting for me to receive support from legislative leadership. A former Speaker of the House who originally led the way to establish our office also accurately summed up the reality we evaluators face by saying, "There's push and pull on OPE and in particular on the director because the outcomes are not always what you were hoping." However, to this day, I wonder if I could have mitigated the situation had I periodically held discussions about the nature of evaluation data and evidence with policymakers.

My third challenge was about the role of evaluation sponsors in deciding or influencing the content of the evaluation report. One way I measure the success of our office is by gauging the use of our evaluations by policymakers, program officials, and other stakeholders. In my efforts to increase use, I had asked JLOC members for their assistance in promoting the work of my office. In response to my request, one of the JLOC co-chairs proposed, among other suggestions, that evaluation reports could be made more useful by "possibly looking at a pre-review meeting to decide whether more work needs to be done on a report before it is released" (Idaho Legislature, 2014a).

Several months later, at a public meeting of JLOC, I briefed the committee on our evaluation process and the professional standards we use in conducting evaluations (Idaho Legislature, 2014b). I again discussed the tension that is always present when we try to be responsive and independent at the same time. In my comments, I expressed serious concerns about JLOC members reviewing draft reports and offering suggestions for making changes to the report before its public release. Participatory data analysis by evaluators and evaluation sponsors may be useful in certain situations. However, it is generally not practiced in a situation like ours where the core function of our office is to conduct independent, nonpartisan oversight evaluations of government policies and programs. I feared such an action would damage the credibility of the report and our office. Even if OPE makes no changes to the report after such a review by JLOC members, there would still be a public perception of compromised OPE independence. A thoughtful discussion followed, but the committee thankfully took no action on the suggestion of previewing our evaluation reports.

However, two weeks later, this JLOC meeting *again* became a media story: "Senator Suggests Secret Review by Lawmakers Before Releasing OPE Reports" (Russell, 2014) and "Idaho Government Evaluators Cautious About Change" (Kruesi, 2014). Once again, had I done a better job of educating JLOC members about our work and the evaluation process, these uncomfortable media headlines might not have appeared.

# LESSONS LEARNED

Being the director of OPE for 15 years has taught me many things. Here are several lessons I have learned that will make my tightrope walking easier in the future.

- **Communicate, communicate, communicate.** When looking back at each of the three challenges I've discussed, clearly a communication gap occurred between me and certain policymakers. I assumed that policymakers understood the nature of our work and the importance of how we do that work, especially how critical evaluator independence is for maintaining credibility. But I failed to devote sufficient time to explaining this to policymakers. In retrospect, this was a big mistake. To be effective in a public policy environment, evaluators should regularly remind policymakers and other stakeholders about the importance of values that we evaluators cherish, such as independence and responsiveness. We also need to remember that new policymakers and stakeholders are constantly coming on the scene because of turnover; newly elected policymakers are likely to be unfamiliar with the nuances of conducting independent evaluations. The bottom line here is that you can never communicate too much with policymakers.

- **Take a walk in policymakers' shoes.** Policymakers are busy folks, and getting their attention isn't easy. Many of us in the public, including evaluators, do not fully appreciate all the competing and conflicting political demands that policymakers are faced with on a regular basis. We can disagree with their policies or approaches, but it would be folly to assume that they have simple tasks with easy solutions on hand. Having gained some maturity in my job, I now believe that effective communication with policymakers is one of the most important and challenging aspects of my job. In my case, this communication is an art form. It requires continuous refinement and involves building relationships, establishing trust, using professional judgment (and yes, some guess work), and hoping for lots of luck.

- **Nurture evaluation champions.** I believe with fostering better communication and trust with policymakers comes the most important and long-lasting benefit, that is, enhancing the chances of converting some of these policymakers from just being users of a specific evaluation to becoming champions of the field of evaluation. These champions will not only improve evaluation use, but they will also help evaluators and evaluation offices everywhere manage the politics of evaluation.

- **Reflect, reflect, reflect.** If we want to learn from the challenges we are presented with as evaluators, we must be introspective. It does not help to argue about what others should or shouldn't have done. For me, the least I can do is to strive for the betterment of my craft because I have the honor and privilege of making government work better for the people of Idaho through evaluation. Finally, I am grateful to all the legislators involved in the three challenges that I experienced. They helped me become a better evaluator.

## REFLECTIVE QUESTIONS

1. To what degree should an evaluation sponsor play a role in deciding the scope of an evaluation?

2. How much of a role should an evaluation sponsor play in deciding the content of an evaluation report?

3. What are some possible ways to gain the attention of busy policy and other decision makers?

## REFERENCES

Dvorak, T. (2013, January 9). Survey shows teachers' worries. *Idaho Statesman*.

Idaho Legislature. (2008, January 16). *Joint Legislative Oversight Committee meeting minutes*. Retrieved from https://legislature.idaho.gov/wp-content/uploads/OPE/JLOCMinutes/min080116.pdf

Idaho Legislature. (2014a, February 27). *Joint Legislative Oversight Committee meeting minutes*. Retrieved from https://legislature.idaho.gov/wp-content/uploads/OPE/JLOCMinutes/min140227.pdf

Idaho Legislature. (2014b, July 14). *Joint Legislative Oversight Committee meeting minutes.* Retrieved from https://legislature.idaho.gov/wp-content/uploads/OPE/JLOCMinutes/min140714.pdf

Kruesi, K. (2014, July 28). Idaho government evaluators cautious about change. *The Washington Times.* Retrieved from http://www.washingtontimes.com/news/2014/jul/28/idaho-government-evaluators-cautious-about-change

Popkey, D. (2013, February 18). Legislature's auditor defends teacher report. *Idaho Statesman.*

Russell, B. (2014, July 28). Senator suggests secret review by lawmakers before releasing OPE reports. *The Spokesman-Review, Eye on Boise.* Retrieved from http://www.spokesman.com/blogs/boise/2014/jul/28/senator-suggests-secret-review-releasing-agency-performance-evaluations

# 8

# WHEN NATIONAL PRIDE IS BEYOND FACTS

## Navigating Conflicting Stakeholder Requirements

## Felix Muramutsa

*Felix Muramutsa, MA Psychology, is a freelance consultant with a background of more than 20 years in evaluation, monitoring, and social research in various domains.*

The accusation was blunt: "How can you act like a foreigner?" It started out as a standard evaluation, but somewhere along the way I began to be treated by some officials as the accomplice of foreigners that wanted to destroy my country's economy! Let me tell you a story that involves navigating the tricky relationships between international donors and government in collecting baseline findings.

## ABOUT ME

My name is Felix Muramutsa. I'm a freelance consultant holding 20 years of experience with more than 30 assignments in research, monitoring and evaluation. I have worked with UN agencies, U.S.-funded projects, international and local nongovernmental organizations (NGOs), civil society organizations, government institutions, foreign and national universities, and the private sector. I have a master's degree in psychology and a bachelor's degree in education.

## DESCRIPTION OF THE EVALUATION

The evaluation I'm about to relate was a baseline prevalence survey of a child labour project run by an international NGO (INGO) for which I was working as senior monitoring and evaluation (M&E) advisor and deputy director. The purpose of the evaluation was to assess the prevalence of child labour in the project's zone of intervention, in order to set up benchmarks and other key indicators of project implementation. The scope of the evaluation was to assess the prevalence of child labour in the country's tea sector prior to project intervention. The major stakeholders were a foreign government donor agency that funded the project, the government (represented by the Ministry of Labour), tea companies, tea cooperatives, district and local authorities, the implementing international organization, local NGOs, and beneficiary parents and children.

My role as the senior M&E advisor was to coordinate the overall baseline survey and ensure the consultancy company hired to conduct it delivered accordingly, respecting the expectations of the donor, INGO, and government. The role of government staff was to ensure the baseline data reflected the local reality. The role of local authorities was to ensure the participation of the sampled population in the survey. The tea companies and cooperatives were involved to ensure the baseline data reflected their attempts at combating child labour in the tea sector. Although there were laws, regulations, and policies in place to prevent child labour, enforcing it was very challenging on the ground. And the role of the implementing partners, including local NGOs and a federation of cooperatives, was to support the evaluation team in their respective zones of intervention.

As the overall baseline coordinator, I had to ensure that all stakeholders' roles and expectations were aligned. I participated in defining the Terms of Reference, selected the consultancy company, and trained and supervised the research team.

I also had the difficult task of liaising between the INGO's headquarters back in the United States, the foreign donor agency, and the government.

## THE MISTAKE OR CHALLENGE

The complication I faced was that the requirements of the donor and the INGO sometimes conflicted with those of the government, and my job as the evaluation facilitator was to respect them all. For example, as the funder of the survey, the donor considered that the baseline results were first and foremost their business only. However, the government also required me to inform them of all the steps occurring and expected me to validate the findings with them prior to publication. In fact, all major household studies such as this one were required to go through an approval process with the National Institute of Statistics and the National Ethics Committee, particularly if children are involved. But I was instructed by my employer (the INGO) to not share the preliminary findings with the government. Instead, they were discussed and validated by the consultancy company, the INGO, and the foreign donor agency. Later on, the INGO shared a final version with the government, and I was tasked to follow up with dissemination.

The alert came when the local NGOs and tea cooperatives started challenging baseline results during meetings with government officials. Tea is a very important product of the country, and the government was worried that a high prevalence of child labour would hamper tea exports and hence the national economy. To my dismay, the government questioned our methodology, sampling, and findings and ultimately rejected the report. I was personally caught in the middle, with each side requiring me to convince the other of their position.

Jana Curll

I believe things went wrong when I failed to question and, instead, accepted instructions from the INGO and donor not to involve the government in all steps of the baseline survey. I should have known there would be complications at the validation stage. What contributed to this mistake was my blind respect of the donor and INGO's request to prioritize their interests before the interests of the government, all the while knowing it conflicted with the government's requirements of being involved at all stages of the project, including the baseline.

There were, however, some factors not under my control. The decision to not share the preliminary findings with the government prior to sharing them with the donor was made by my employer, the INGO. If I had chosen to ignore their instructions, I would have been in breach of my contract. But informing my employer of the government's expectations was under my control. I did it, but only informally and probably not sufficiently. When things began to go wrong, I became a scapegoat. I was very frustrated to be treated by certain government officials as an accomplice of "foreigners that want to destroy the country's economy by exaggerating a fake child labour prevalence." I was shocked, as I knew that was not at all my intention!

To address the situation, I held a number of personal conversations in and out of the office with government officials and other key players to better understand the problem. I learned that it was not a methodological issue, but rather a fear of how the report would be perceived by higher officials. We discussed what improvements needed to be made to the draft report and what could be reviewed and/or presented differently. Nevertheless, it was a dilemma, and I continued to struggle with selecting which information to disclose to which side and the best way to reach a compromise.

Although the baseline survey was conducted and completed in 2014, it was not validated until the end of the project in April 2017. The situation worsened to become more than a technical issue between the INGO, donor, and the government. In fact, in the end the donor had to engage their own embassy to resolve the issue with the national government as a bilateral political issue.

# LESSONS LEARNED

Thinking back on this situation, there are several things I would have done differently to avoid these mistakes.

- **Involve all stakeholders.** As an evaluator, this awful situation has influenced my work significantly as it has sharpened me to better understand that the early involvement and active participation of all stakeholders is key for a successful evaluation. More involvement from stakeholders would have helped me to assess everyone's expectations, plus anticipate and resolve any conflicting agendas.

- **Set up a steering committee.** In retrospect, I should have pushed to set up a joint baseline steering committee. The role of the steering committee would be to anticipate and discuss any issues that might surface at all levels: technical, administrative, or political, including contractual issues that might limit the evaluation.

- **Advocate when necessary.** Ensure that the donors and local government have the same understanding of the evaluation's terms of reference, objectives, methodology, and preliminary findings. Be active in advocating and pushing donors to understand local government and authorities' requirements and expectations and, conversely, help local government and authorities to accommodate donor and INGO deadlines and deliverables. It's a continuous and balancing role for any evaluator.

# REFLECTIVE QUESTIONS

1. Why do you think the international donor and INGO insisted on viewing the results prior to the government? How do you think the evaluator could have addressed this situation more proactively?

2. How can evaluators balance conflicting expectations and requirements in general between donors, employers and/or contractors, and the recipient government?

3. What protective measures might support an evaluator in the middle of conflicting stakeholder agendas?

# 9

# STARS IN OUR EYES

## What Happens When Things Are Too Good to Be True

### Jara Dean-Coffey

*Jara Dean-Coffey, MPH, Luminare Group's fearless and funny founder, has spent more than twenty-five years working with leaders who hold one thing in common: a commitment to challenging themselves and their organizations to have a transformative impact on the individuals, communities, and systems they touch.*

think evaluative thinking capacity building is so important that I do it even when the organization doesn't ask for it. So when I get a client who says they are interested in it, I get all starry-eyed. However, as you'll see, sometimes the stars in our eyes get in the way of being able to clearly see red flags that are there from the start.

## ABOUT ME

I'm Jara Dean-Coffey. I have worked with foundations, nonprofits, and the public sector for more than twenty years, primarily serving in an external capacity. Luminare Group, the company I founded in 2002 (formerly jdcPartnerships), offers three lines of service: consulting (strategy formation and planning & evaluation), capacity building (primarily evaluative thinking), and pushing practice (emerging issues relevant to evaluative practice: intersection of leadership, strategy, and evaluation). Our client partners engage in addressing structural and systemic barriers that limit the health and well-being of those people who are most marginalized in the United States. It is deeply rewarding work.

After about ten years of working as a consultant, I knew that something wasn't right about how evaluation translated for organizations. Often when we arrived as consultants, clients were unable to answer simple questions like "What would be different if this worked?" "Can you tell me how these activities connect to each other?" and "Do you know what part of your program is the most important to keep?" They expected us to be the experts on how their organization or program worked. And as an engagement came to an end, they didn't seem to be better able to make the link among intention, inquiry, and information. They were, in fact, no better off than before we worked with them. It was incredibly frustrating and disheartening.

I was lucky enough to have a class with Dr. Rosalie Torres and became familiar with the writing around evaluative thinking. Evaluative thinking is "a type of reflective practice that integrates the same skills that characterize good evaluation—asking questions of substance, determining what data are required to answer specific questions, collecting data using appropriate strategies, analyzing collected data and summarizing findings, and using the findings—throughout all of an organization's work practices."[1] Suddenly, a light went on; I had found the missing link! Since then, evaluative thinking capacity building has been a core part of how we conceptualize and engage in working with our clients.

## DESCRIPTION OF THE EVALUATION

We were approached by a federally funded national coalition to make its evaluation work more meaningful by strengthening its evaluative thinking muscles.

---

[1] Breuner Foundation. (2014–2015). *Evaluative thinking*. Retrieved from http://www.evaluativethinking .org/evalthink.html

The coalition was a five-year project that had more than 600 partners across 44 U.S. states and the 6 Pacific Island territories/jurisdictions. It represented clinics, other coalitions, state and local health departments, policy makers, and academic institutions in rural and urban areas, as well as an advisory board. As you can see from the scale of the operation, evaluative thinking capacity building was more than a simple notion, but we were excited by the possibilities.

We had the opportunity with a new initiative they were launching to build some evaluative thinking practices through capacity building. Our experience was that by intentionally engaging organizations in thinking about the questions they wanted to answer for themselves about their work and/or the statements they wanted to be able to make about their work, they start to think differently about data. They start to think about questions, assumptions, and intentions. They begin to make clearer and cleaner links among what they do, why they do it, who they do it for, how they do it, and what they hope will change as a consequence.

As part of its funding requirements, the coalition had to submit data regularly through a federally developed online reporting tool. Coalition partners found the tool cumbersome, and the data it required them to submit did not convey the depth and breadth of their efforts and impact. In short, the data they were submitting had little value or relevance for them. Coalition partners wanted something more meaningful and engaging. They knew what they wanted but did not know where to start in terms of (1) rethinking the relationship between what they said they would do and were actually doing, (2) being more explicit about what they hoped their efforts would accomplish, (3) clarifying and prioritizing the questions they had about their work and its effects, and (4) determining the most relevant information they needed. They needed help. They called us.

We know a client has the potential to be the right one for evaluative thinking capacity building if they call us with an understanding of what they don't know and want to be able to do better on their own. Also, because many of the coalition partners were smaller grassroots nonprofits engaged in social justice work, there was an opportunity to reach an audience that often does not get access to what we have to offer. The stars were shining brightly in our eyes.

Our contract was to be for three years, with the first year focusing on clarity and framing. This meant working with our client to articulate their program design more explicitly (through a logic model) and then beginning the process of working with them

Jana Curll

and their partners to determine what questions they had, what information they were already collecting to answer those questions, and how it aligned with the information they were reporting to the federal government. Once we were all on the same page in terms of understanding the coalition's existing information practices, we could begin to build new practices, determine if new information was needed, and figure out why and how the information would be collected and utilized (for the coalition, for reporting, and for the coalition partners).

Knowing this was to be a multiyear relationship, we plotted a scope of work that would build greater evaluation capacity each year focusing primarily on our client, the coalition, with more and more of the responsibility and thinking transferring to them over time. The initial meetings with the project director and project manager were great in that we were able to articulate the big picture goals of the coalition and map out, at least initially, how the various partners were to contribute to making these goals a reality. This would provide the foundation for refining data collection tools and determining how to engage coalition partners in sensemaking so they had ownership of the data and could bring nuances and context to the analysis that we could not. One of our tasks was to make recommendations for refining a data management tool. We would create a reporting template that would both feed the federal online reporting tool as well as meet other information and communication needs of our client and the coalition partners. We would do this in partnership with the coalition and its partners. Our role was to bring framing and focus to their inquiry so that it helped them (1) make sense of the data being collected, (2) institute practices that supported shared analysis, and (3) use findings to advance the coalition's goals for the initiative as well as that of its individual partners. We were clear, and had agreement, that we would not be the face of this work but be behind the scenes, offering recommendations, resources, coaching, and support. It was EXACTLY the type of work we dream about. Ah, dreams . . .

After the initial meeting, our primary contact was the project manager, who had research and evaluation experience. We created a work plan, including check-ins. We mutually agreed that at the end of Year 1 we would review progress, set a new set of objectives, and continue strengthening the national coalition's capacity to think evaluatively, modifying the focus of their inquiry as needed. It was a strong start.

## THE MISTAKE OR CHALLENGE

Things began well enough. We worked with the program manager and a program assistant to refine the program model to better highlight the connections between their role as a national coalition and their regional coalition partners. We also identified key data collection tools to be developed or refined over the course of the five-year project.

I cringe when I think back about this, but it soon became clear that we made several mistakes early on in the project. The first oversight was that we didn't inquire much about the evaluation capacity of the coalition's partners or the strength of their existing data collection and data management tools. Then we did something you should never do: we made an assumption. We assumed that the coalition had previous experience collecting data of this nature from their partners and that we would only be refining what was already in place. We were wrong. This was not the case.

My first sense that this was going to be an issue came after a team member participated in a webinar to review the federal online reporting tool for the project. The level of detail of the data that the federal agency expected the coalition to capture was higher than we had anticipated. This, coupled with the realization that the coalition (as many do) typically obtained information only through the use of partners' narrative reports and/or verbal updates, made it clear that our initial proposal to "make recommendations for refining a data management tool" (our reporting template) would become "develop a full-blown data management tool." At this point, we should have renegotiated the original terms of the contract for a larger scope and asked for more money, but we didn't. Oh, and if we didn't have enough challenges already, the project director left. Red flags were everywhere.

However, despite this significant change in scope, we still had stars in our eyes and thought evaluative thinking capacity building was feasible. We felt that despite these changes, we could still develop an internal tool that could support coalition partners to collect information that was both useful to themselves and supported meeting the federal online reporting requirements. So we shifted gears and modified our original reporting template into a user-friendly internal data management and reporting tool using an online survey platform. This tool allowed the coalition partners to get a full sense of what the coalition was being asked to report to federal funders and walked them through submitting data that would align with these requirements. This shift in our role should have been a one-off departure from the original contract except that the program manager took a new job soon after our tool was launched. We ended up unexpectedly serving as the data maven during the transition, putting us further over budget. Another red flag.

A new program director was hired who was also assigned the role of interim program manager. This individual excelled in cultivating connections and a shared vision among the coalition partners, but unlike her predecessor, did not have experience in research or evaluation. Our internal data management tool, while friendly on the data entry side, still required a fair amount of manipulation to extract, aggregate, and cross-tabulate as needed to fulfill the federal reporting obligations and provide usable, useful summary information for the coalition and its partners. Unfortunately, the interim program manager was not able to fulfill this role. This was turning into a hot mess.

Our second oversight was that we didn't consider that national politics would put these federally funded projects under increased scrutiny. Given the changes in staffing and the higher-stakes accountability that came with the political climate, we eventually took on the role of leading the data collection and analysis entirely and preparing summaries that the coalition could easily translate into the federal reporting tool. Once again, we were working outside the original scope. We had put ourselves in this position by failing to adjust to the earlier unanticipated internal shifts that continued to place work on our shoulders. We were annoyed at ourselves and felt trapped, but because of the importance of the coalition's work and how it aligned with our values, we continued working on the project.

Over the course of the next year, three program managers (and three program assistants) came and went, and with each transition went the knowledge and understanding of our data management tool. Our connection to the program director and coalition partners kept us talking about evaluative thinking and bringing these concepts to bear whenever we prepared and reviewed summaries, talked about challenges to collecting data, or discussed strategies for enhancing program impact. However, we kept banking on eventually being able to hand off the labor-intensive task of data analysis and summarizing to someone else at the coalition so we could get back to the real work of evaluative thinking capacity building.

However, despite our original intentions, we were never quite able to serve as an evaluative thinking coach. The timing of so many staff departures and arrivals relative to the coalition's reporting deadlines had us scrambling to make sure the organization had what they needed for reporting. We were never able to sufficiently re-scope or fully assess the challenges and determine what we needed to adjust to switch to an evaluative thinking capacity building role or if that was even feasible. We became quasi-staff. This can be a great thing for an external evaluator—to truly be a part of the team. However, there is always a risk with a small budget and small team. The significant staff turnover created a situation where we, the evaluator took on responsibilities and held institutional knowledge that exceeded what an external evaluator should hold. This combination of factors often leads to working hours that don't get billed. That was certainly the case in this situation. As evaluators, we understand and often accept there is some degree of pro bono work that happens, particularly with this type of engagement. However, this situation went beyond our comfort zone.

As we neared the end of Year 2, we found ourselves engaged in designing, conducting, and analyzing additional interviews with coalition partners as a means to contextualize some of the data gathered through the online tool. We did this partly because we were still trying to build the evaluative thinking capacity of our client even though we knew they did not have the staffing stability to receive what we had to offer. Thinking back, the coalition was always satisfied (grateful even) with our work and commitment. We ended up creating internal drama and tension amongst ourselves as a team because we could never quite get to the type of evaluative thinking engagement we had hoped for in the beginning. We were still holding on to the dream of one day being the evaluative thinking capacity builder, so we embarked on this interview process in a manner that would allow us to hand it off one day. In short, we created an interview toolkit. Guess what? This put us further over budget.

After we reviewed the summary of interviews with coalition staff, they surprised us with the announcement of yet another staff transition. I knew at this point there was only one thing we could do. We finally let go of our evaluative thinking capacity building dreams and ended the engagement a year early.

# LESSONS LEARNED

I still get a little starry-eyed and hopeful when a potential client approaches us about intentional evaluative thinking capacity building, but now we do a few things differently.

- **More than interest and willingness are required.** Nowadays we ask questions about the stability of the organization, staffing, their culture of inquiry, and data environment. We seek to understand both their readiness and capacity. If the organization is not currently in a position to engage effectively and consistently in evaluative thinking capacity building work, we explore what role we might play in the interim.

- **Role and scope boundaries are essential.** Although the staff transitions amplified tensions in this project, those transitions didn't have to impact the project the way they did. Ultimately our own desire to be of value prevented us from accurately assessing the client's capacity and creating a scope of work that made sense for both of us. We now have a standard addendum in all our contracts where we explicitly lay out expectations for the client and which the client must sign. If the client's ability to partner, communicate, and/or deliver changes, our scope and timeline will change as well.

- **An evaluation working group is a must.** One key to building evaluation capacity is having it rooted within the organization. By limiting our interactions to one or two staff, we had to keep starting over when they left. In this particular instance, we should have made sure that the program director and perhaps a member or two of the advisory board were part of our core team. This way our discussions, learnings, and decisions would not have resided in the head of only the project manager and suffered from the continual staff turnover.

- **Present a realistic budget and pay attention to changes in scope and modify accordingly.** In the early stages of evaluative thinking capacity building, we are both doing and teaching evaluation. There have to be sufficient resources to engage in the evaluative work itself as well as ways to translate the thinking and decisions for the client so that they understand the evaluative thought process. This requires not only verbal communication but also documentation such as tools and guides that can serve as a reference for others. The efficiencies that come with having an evaluative thinking culture arise after that culture has begun to flourish, not during its cultivation. It takes more time (and thus money) to make the evaluative thinking behind recommendations and insights transparent and accessible to staff to support learning. At the beginning of the project we promised more than we could deliver, and as the work unfolded we dug ourselves into a hole.

# REFLECTIVE QUESTIONS

1.  Building evaluative thinking capacity is a team sport. How can you assess if there are internal champions, interested parties, and the organizational capacity to do so?

2.  Given that staffing often changes, what might we have done differently so that the core of the work remained internal (with the client) as opposed to external (with us)?

3.  What are some indicators that an organization is effectively practicing evaluative thinking?

# 10

# A "FAILED" LOGIC MODEL

## How I Learned to Connect
## With All Stakeholders

## Chris Lovato

*Chris Lovato, PhD, CE, is a Professor in the School of Population & Public Health, Faculty of Medicine, The University of British Columbia in Vancouver, British Columbia, Canada.*

After presenting the logic model we developed, I was stunned when the funder looked directly at me, then turned to the program director and emphatically stated, "These outcomes are *not* what we are funding you to do!" Everyone in the room sat so silent, you could have heard a pin drop. This chapter tells the story of how a technically uncomplicated logic model led to embarrassment for me and serious stakeholder disagreement.

## ABOUT ME

As a graduate student, I took several courses in program evaluation from Professor Karen Kirkhart, at The University of Texas in Austin. Her enthusiasm was contagious, and she sparked in me a commitment that has lasted throughout my 30-year career in public health and evaluation. My career in academia has involved teaching, conducting research, and administering university-based programs. Within these roles I have served as an internal and external evaluator, taught evaluation, and mentored many students.

## DESCRIPTION OF THE EVALUATION

While I was in one of my positions as an internal evaluator, I was pleased when a program director within the organization requested my group to plan an evaluation. The program of interest was a university-based, provincially funded initiative designed to facilitate international medical graduates in enhancing their skills and preparing for physician licensing exams. The project had been ongoing for several years and was to be expanded with new monies available via the federal government. The purpose of the evaluation was to gather information regarding implementation and program outcomes in order to inform ongoing improvements and for purposes of external accountability. The initial evaluation was to take place over a period of three years, with plans to put a system in place for ongoing evaluation over the long term. The stakeholders included program enrollees, university administrators, program staff, and the funder. At the time, I was the director of the evaluation unit responsible for evaluating medical education programs, and my role was to lead the evaluation with the help of an evaluation assistant from my unit.

Following the standard practice of beginning our evaluation by connecting with stakeholders, the evaluation assistant and I met with the university administrator who was responsible for overseeing the program. The evaluation assistant then met with the faculty member and program staff who were running the program. With their input, and with reference to the program proposal and negotiated contract, we worked together to develop a draft logic model that was quite straightforward and appeared to have all the qualities of a "good" logic model. Using a series of boxes and arrows, it depicted the program and showed the relationships between resources, activities, outputs, and outcomes. Within our organization there were unwritten norms that contact with government funders should only be initiated by the university administration, unless otherwise arranged. Therefore, in this case, as evaluators, we did not meet with the government representative responsible for this program.

Having developed the logic model, we prepared to present it to stakeholders. I expected there might be some revisions to the model, but I felt confident we had put something together that accurately described the program. Evaluation was one of the first items on the agenda for a program advisory group meeting that was made up of high-level policy and decision makers, including university administrators, the program director, various department heads, representatives from the government agency funding the program, the evaluation assistant, and me.

## THE MISTAKE OR CHALLENGE

At the advisory group meeting, I took the lead in describing the draft logic model. Following my presentation, there was complete silence. I looked around the table. Then the government funder spoke up. He looked directly at me, then the program director, and emphatically stated, "These outcomes are *not* what we are funding you to do!" I was stunned. Not sure what to say, a number of questions raced through my mind. How did this happen? Where did I go wrong? I was mortified and wasn't sure what my next step would be. The room remained silent and still for what seemed like an eternity. Then there was a brief discussion, which made it abundantly clear the program developers and the funder were not on the same page. The program director finally spoke up and said, "We'll have to table this for now and discuss it off-line. Let's move to the next agenda item."

That was that. I sat through the rest of the meeting and tried hard to sit up straight so no one would guess how embarrassed I felt. Here I was, an evaluator with many years of experience and the senior evaluator on the project; I had embarrassed not only myself but also the evaluation assistant I was working with. I had also succeeded in making the program director (a colleague) and the university look bad. For days following the meeting, the voice in my head kept repeating, "If you were a good evaluator, this wouldn't have happened!"

That was more than seven years ago. Since then, I've moved on to doing other things, but the evaluation we started is still going strong. With some fairly minor revisions, the "failed" logic model was used and actually led to some very productive conversations between the university and the government funder. They ultimately came to an agreement about the program's outcomes, and the evaluation has proven to be useful for making program improvements and demonstrating accountability. Some changes were made to the original logic model to reflect ongoing discussions. An ongoing evaluation has been set in place and a logic model that reflects changes made over time lives on, with even more revisions anticipated in the future as the program continues to develop.

# LESSONS LEARNED

- **Engage all levels of stakeholders.** This was a good lesson on the value of connecting with all stakeholders in the process of drafting a logic model. It now seems obvious to me that an initial meeting with the funder would have quickly identified the problem with the outcomes. I could have even sent a draft of the logic model for comment prior to the meeting, which might have led to a "pre-meeting" discussion. The logic model itself is only half the product—the other half is the process.

- **Be attuned to your personal biases.** Ongoing reflective practice and awareness of your biases is key to a successful evaluation. As an internal evaluator, I had overidentified with the organization I was working for and hadn't considered what would have been the more objective approach of making arrangements to also speak with a key stakeholder—the program funder. The logic model reflected only the perspective of the program designers and implementers. At the time, I felt constrained by the unwritten rule that only higher-level university administrators could communicate with the government. I later learned that this wasn't an issue at all; I just needed to go through the proper channels. Over time, we developed strong working relationships with the government representatives who funded us. This was significant in developing evaluation plans for other projects that were meaningful to all stakeholders involved.

- **Logic models are a tool that facilitate understanding.** Evaluators help program directors and decision makers get clear about their program and identify what they are working to achieve. Logic models are a stepping stone toward that goal. Identifying the miscommunication between those running the program and the funder at an early stage in the evaluation is a *good* thing.

- **Keep your perspective.** Finally, I also learned to keep things in perspective and set aside my ego. As evaluators, we engage stakeholders and develop draft logic models for a reason—it's highly unlikely that the first version of the logic model presented to stakeholders will ever be the last! Sometimes you will not have the right information, or you may misinterpret the information. And sometimes stakeholders don't agree or aren't clear about what should be in the logic model. As an evaluator, I found myself in a very awkward and uncomfortable situation; however, in addition to my personal learning, my oversight uncovered an important issue that needed to be dealt with by the key stakeholders. In the end, the changes that were made led to positive results.

## REFLECTIVE QUESTIONS

1. It is ideal to involve all stakeholders in developing a logic model, but what if, for some reason, this is not possible? What options might you consider if circumstances are such that you are not able to communicate with all stakeholders before presenting a draft logic model?

2. Logic models are most frequently discussed when a program is being evaluated. How can a logic model also be useful during the program planning and implementation phases?

3. How might the process of developing a logic model differ for an internal versus an external evaluator? What are the advantages and disadvantages of each?

# 11

# LOST WITHOUT YOU

## A Lesson in System Mapping and Engaging Stakeholders

Josh Berson Photography

## Kylie Hutchinson

*Kylie Hutchinson, BSc, CE, is an independent evaluation con-sultant and trainer with Community Solutions Planning & Eval-uation, based in Vancouver, British Columbia.*

The room became deadly quiet. As I looked around the meeting table, I was met by a dozen blank stares. "I don't get it," someone finally said. My heart sank as I realized my first attempt at drawing a system map was a complete failure.

## ABOUT ME

I discovered evaluation via an undergraduate course and thesis and was immediately hooked. My first few jobs were managing nonprofit programs, but whenever a manager learned that I had an evaluation background, I was given an extra evaluation assignment to complete. I eventually decided to go out on my own as an independent evaluation consultant. Thirty years later, I still love doing evaluation, evaluation capacity building, and developing practical resources for evaluators.

## DESCRIPTION OF THE EVALUATION

One of my more recent contracts was to provide ongoing evaluation support to a high-level committee formed to address a challenging issue in British Columbia's health care system. The committee met monthly, and the longer I sat at this table, the more I realized how incredibly complex this issue was. I wanted to capture the complexity of the system surrounding this issue. I thought that if I took the initiative to communicate this complexity somehow, it would help the committee think more strategically, plus help to inform the boundaries of the evaluation. So, I automatically thought of a system map. A *system* is a group of interconnected elements that function, and are viewed, as part of a greater whole. A program is part of a system, or can be a system in itself. The issue this committee was addressing was clearly influenced by elements in the system surrounding it. I chose to do a system map because of its ability to visualize what's going on in the system and potential places to intervene. Unlike the usually linear logic model, a system map explores how different parts of the system are interconnected and can better portray things like other actors, different interrelationships, flows, and feedback loops. There are different kinds of system maps, such as actor maps and mind maps, but I chose to draw a variation of a causal loop diagram that illustrated positive and negative influences on the issue in question in terms of circular cause-and-effect loops (Figure 11.1).

I was very excited to have my first compelling reason to draw a system map and delighted that I would be able to provide the committee with something they'd find extremely useful. The following week I spent several days sequestered in my office happily developing my system map, and when it was complete, I felt a deep satisfaction. The process of identifying all the parts of the system and interconnections was extremely enjoyable and the days flew by as I worked in blissful concentration. I drew everything that I considered a barrier as a red arrow and everything that was an enabler in blue. As I was doing this, I had a number of unexpected insights regarding the system surrounding the issue, as well as possible strategies and potential leverage

**FIGURE 11.1 ■ My original system map.**

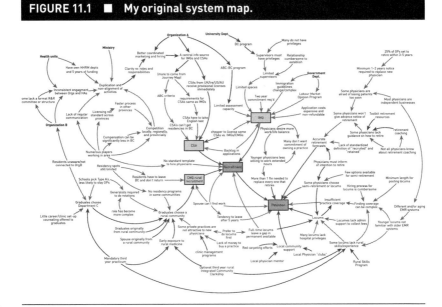

*Source:* Kylie Hutchinson

points for further action. At times, it felt like these insights were jumping off the page at me. When I finished, it was abundantly clear to me where the committee needed to intervene, and I believed that once they saw it themselves, they would realize it, too.

It was so simple!

# THE MISTAKE OR CHALLENGE

Come the day of our meeting, I could barely contain my anticipation. I proudly printed out the map on 11" × 17" paper and set it down as a placemat at each member's seat before people began to arrive. I wanted to ensure that members had extra time to review it before the meeting started.

When it came time to present, I excitedly walked members through an onscreen version of the map, then gazed around the table prepared to facilitate deep and meaningful discussion on the issue. To my surprise, I was met instead by a room full of blank stares. Members mumbled things like "Uh, it's kind of overwhelming," some looked at me like I was from outer space, and others avoided my gaze altogether. One person finally asked if I could put the map into a table format for easier comprehension. Sigh. I slunk back to my seat and sat in embarrassed silence.

However, not to be deterred, I enlarged it as a full-size poster for the next meeting, thinking maybe it was just a readability problem. If they only saw it

Jana Curll

bigger, they'd understand its true genius! But they still didn't use it. Now it's just hanging on the wall in my office, staring at me daily.

Later that year at a virtual conference held by the American Evaluation Association's Systems in Evaluation Topical Interest Group, I joined a breakout group on Tools & Strategies for Systems Visualization and told my tale of woe. Upon hearing my story, one of the other participants observed, "Maybe system maps are a better investigative tool than a communications tool?" It then dawned on me that my original approach for developing a system map was all wrong. Only through drawing the map myself was I able to fully understand the complexity inherent in the issue, but from my perspective only.

I realized that it was the practice of me thinking through the different barriers and enablers myself that made the leverage points and strategies so easy for me, but not for my stakeholders, to see. Put another way, it was the *process* of producing the map that yielded the insights, not simply staring at the *product*. Not only had I neglected to consider that understanding different stakeholder perspectives is a cornerstone of systems thinking, I'd also forgotten that engaging stakeholders is also a critical part of effective evaluation practice. I had a map, but I was lost without my stakeholders.

## LESSONS LEARNED

- **Don't do it alone.** Systems are conceptual notions of how we make sense of an interconnected world. But stakeholders have different perspectives, so it's important to blend these perspectives. Doing it together helps to work towards consensus on things such as the boundaries of the system; interrelationships, connections, and patterns among various elements in the system; plus different views on how the system functions. If you want to use a system map to visualize and navigate complexity, develop it *with* a group of stakeholders, not *for* them. Drawing it collaboratively helps people to improve their overall grasp and shared understanding of the system. They can better appreciate what's happening, identify root problems, and discover strategic leverage points.

- **They don't have to be slick.** System maps don't have to be fancy; they just have to be meaningful and useful to those who produced them. One drawn with flipchart paper and markers can be just as effective as an interactive digital version if it yields valuable insights and prompts action.

- **Consider a rich picture instead.** Although system maps are a form of visualization, a page full of arrows and labels isn't the most engaging or memorable of images. Next time I'm going to try a similar but slightly different approach to mapping called a rich picture (Figure 11.2). A rich picture is a drawing of a complex situation that integrates different stakeholder perspectives into one picture but differs from a system map in that it can explicitly include issues such as conflict, emotions, and politics.

## REFLECTIVE QUESTIONS

1. How might an evaluator engage busy stakeholders in a collaborative system mapping process?

2. What are some other ways that evaluators can help stakeholders appreciate the complexity present in a system?

3. What other parts of the evaluation cycle might the lessons in this chapter apply to?

**FIGURE 11.2 ■ A rich picture can integrate different stakeholder perspectives into one picture, and explicitly show how things like conflict, emotions, and politics influence an issue.**

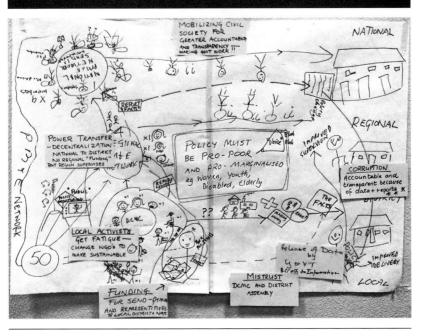

*Source:* Steve Waddell (2012).

# 12

# YOU GOT TO KNOW WHEN TO HOLD 'EM

## An Evaluation That Went From Bad to Worse

Robert P. Shepherd

*Robert P. Shepherd, PhD, CE, is an associate professor in the School of Public Policy & Administration at Carleton University in Ottawa, Ontario, Canada.*

Whenever I think of one particular evaluation, that old Kenny Rogers tune, "The Gambler," plays in my head: "You got to know when to hold 'em, know when to fold 'em." Negotiating the terms of the evaluation seemed to start off so well, but four months into the project, I could not fathom how things had turned so badly. I am sure I sustained some reputational damage, not to mention the feeling that I had failed at something I always believed to be true: that I know how to guide and motivate people and relationships. How did I get here? Was there anything I could have done differently?

## ABOUT ME

My name is Robert Shepherd. I consider myself a relative newcomer to academia, having joined the School of Public Policy & Administration at Carleton University in July 2007. I supervise the graduate Diploma in Public Policy & Program Evaluation, and conduct much research in governmental evaluation policy, applying this experience to larger issues of public management. Having spent many years inside and outside government, evaluation has been a mainstay of my professional and academic life, lessons that I bring to my teaching and mentoring of graduate students.

## DESCRIPTION OF THE EVALUATION

As the graduate supervisor, part of my role is to solicit support from government departments and nonprofit organizations to sponsor evaluation practicum projects that graduate students might be able to work on over the course of their diploma program. I prefer to work with small departments and agencies, as often they are more invested in their programs and are better able to make the effort to work with students and give them guidance when needed.

Preparing for a fall intake of students, I approached a colleague and friend of mine in government about the possibility of his department sponsoring one such project. Over the course of a few meetings over lunch, we devised a project based on a real need the department was trying to address. The program was a federal communications and outreach program designed with the twin objectives of creating awareness of the department's mandate and responsibilities as these relate to public servants and to promote use of their services if and when they were needed by individuals. The department was still reeling after having experienced several ethical breaches along the way by key people in leadership positions that attracted significant media attention. The department was also the subject of targeted audits by the auditor general and the termination of some key personnel. This was a department that already felt unfairly targeted and has a very difficult time trusting "outsiders" with their information and experience. Knowing this at the time should have been enough for me to stay clear of exposing students to this culture of distrust. We knew this was the case when we explored the project, which is why "trust" was considered a major element of the evaluation.

Trusting in my own ability to manage relationships, I decided to move ahead in any case. The evaluation's aim was initially to assess communications tools such as brochures, website materials, communiques, and other written instruments. The agreement was that this may be an appropriate beginning, but if the students observed deeper issues these would be evaluated as well. The students began to prepare an inception report containing questions and methods related to understanding how better to reach public servants. It did not take long to learn that the success of the department was highly dependent on building trust with public servants. So important is the trust relationship that the department would simply not be able to perform without it. The students came to this conclusion very early on, and they made a strong case that the evaluation should focus on assessing the department's efforts at building trust through its most outward face: the communications and outreach program.

In our scoping conversations with senior departmental officials, there appeared to be a general acceptance of this approach. The students built a brilliant theory of change, with trust as its dependent variable, and proceeded to construct a theory-based approach that would test key assumptions central to creating the conditions needed for trust to be established between the department and individual public servants.

Everything looked hopeful to this point, but it all went downhill from there.

# THE MISTAKE OR CHALLENGE

The students and I were asked to present the plan to the department's Audit Committee comprising high-powered individuals including the deputy minister. The room was full of good intentions and the desire to assist the students in any way they could. But, it was also clear the committee was uncomfortable with the proposed approach. Departmental executives could see the merit of the evaluation plan. However, the program staff believed the students were well outside their original mandate. Despite various reminders that evaluations are dynamic and that original diagnoses change, the program staff were adamant in their view that the students should focus only on the original, narrowly defined evaluation questions. Although not obvious at the time, I realize now that the program staff did not wish to seem incompetent in front of the Audit Committee. In hindsight the students and I understood we could have done much more to engage the program staff and bring them into that meeting as supporters of the evaluation rather than the slighted cynics they were.

It did not help that departmental executives could also see the discomfort of the program staff, plus the worried looks on the faces of the Audit Committee members that the plan had not sold well. It should have come as no surprise to me when the deputy minister said, "We will want to see this evaluation plan fully laid out, with key people you wish to speak with identified. And, we will want to approve every sentence in the evaluation plan you submit within 30 days." I knew that the students were uncomfortable, but more importantly, as an experienced evaluator, I also knew what this meeting was about at that point. They wanted this project terminated, but for the sake of the students there was some willingness to let things proceed despite some discomfort, which is not always a bad thing. That said, all I could think about was the work the students invested to get to this point and how badly I misread the situation by trusting in my colleague and friend to advocate for the process and the learning exercise.

To make matters even worse, the next day we decided as a team to meet the demands of the committee. I ignored the red firecrackers going off in my head and the hairs standing up on the back of my neck. I asked the students how they felt about moving ahead, and they seemed confident. Meanwhile, I was wrestling with the decision to walk away. We persevered instead.

My fears quickly became reality. Program staff put up several barriers and stalled any progress on the evaluation plan. Requests for information took a long time to fulfill. Calls for assistance from other stakeholder groups were ignored, likely as a result of the unenthusiastic demonstrations of support from the departmental executives. And, I received half-hearted but directive messages from my colleague and friend that the evaluation needed to change course. As it was, the project was already behind schedule, and the students were concerned they would not meet their obligations.

In short, it was a mess. The Kenny Rogers tune was growing louder in my head: "Know when to fold 'em . . ."

Ultimately, my colleague and friend took the bull by the horns and sent an emissary to my office to terminate the project. The decision was made for me and the students. It should not have gotten that far.

Given the late date in the student year, I decided that the students should continue to work on the project as a theoretic exercise and interview other public servants in my network. This helped to inform the direction of the evaluation, and in the end, the students pulled off their final presentation and report with grace and professionalism. Visitors to the presentation were very impressed with their approach and findings. And, the students gained the unique experience of working with a challenging client, a silver lining in a difficult journey.

The road travelled was fraught with many obstacles, and it was clear that the "learning space" for the students was anything but safe. It was my job to provide that safety. As with any critical failures, one learns important lessons and makes corrections.

# LESSONS LEARNED

Thinking back over the course of this project, I learned several lessons that have since informed not only my supervision of student projects but also my own management of evaluation projects.

- **Organizational health and willingness of the client are really important.** The executives and staff of this department were reluctant to trust outsiders and only did so based on my friendship with one of their staff and, to a large extent, on the promise that their very specific needs would be met. As an academic, I know that students should be given the room to explore and test drive the concepts they are learning. But, it is now painfully clear that the same assumptions cannot be applied to clients, who have very different and often parochial expectations of the work being done. This was a sensitive client. Taking stock of organizational willingness and readiness is critical to evaluation success.

- **Building trust with evaluation stakeholders is critical.** It was ironic that a key objective of the department was to build trust with potential users of their services, but trust was given tentatively to the student evaluators. We always had a feeling that departmental officials were wary the students would somehow turn on them. And, if one is perched to find wrong, no matter how small, it should have come as no surprise that when the student evaluators made small mistakes, program staff constructed barriers to justify locking them out. Spending time on relationship building is not a waste of time.

- **Explaining your evaluation plan clearly is critical to obtaining organizational support.** Any rational actor knows this in order to be successful in project management, and every good evaluator knows this too. The students were proud of their work (with good reason). And, I was proud of them for making a sound diagnosis of the program. But, the organization was not ready to hear the diagnosis or the plan to test it. Rather than justifying requests for information and access, and doggedly following the evaluation plan, we could have made sure the plan had support from the beginning and that the client understood clearly what the benefits would be to them following it. What may seem obvious to you may not seem obvious to the client based on the client's own readiness, capacity, and willingness to accept some uncomfortable messages no matter how accurate they may be.

- **Creating a safe space to carry out an evaluation is paramount.** This was a challenging client, and the program being evaluated was not straightforward to assess. People were sensitive about their roles and responsibilities, and this was evident in our interactions. I should have taken time to create a safe space not just for the students but for the client as well. It is not easy to be evaluated by "outsiders," especially within an unhealthy organizational culture. I should have spent more effort on creating a space where everyone could be valued and heard. Evaluation is a human exercise.

- **Know when to walk away.** That old Kenny Rogers tune never stopped playing in my head: "Know when to walk away, and know when to run." Although leaving a client should be used as a last resort, it is nonetheless an option. As evaluators, we often let our own pride and abilities guide our decisions. I also accepted my colleague and friend's assurances that we would be able to work through the challenges. Unfortunately, this was not the case. Evaluation is about relationships, and it comprises dedicated people doing the work. More than one sign was given to walk away when it was clear the department was not at a good point to accept the effort. I should have stopped at the first sign, properly assessed what was happening, and then made the best decision for the students and for me. When Kenny Rogers plays, pay attention.

- **Don't work with your friends.** The old adage "Don't work for your family" applies equally for friends. Relationships are deeply personal, and your own credibility is put on the line when things appear to go wrong. Friends are terrific for making introductions or opening doors for you, but it is something different to work for them. Friends only see the relationship and have a difficult time separating your professional work from that. Not only did the project not work optimally for the students, but I also lost a friend.

## REFLECTIVE QUESTIONS

1. What might be some indicators that an organization is willing, ready, and committed to work through a challenging evaluation project? What conditions would have to be in place to demonstrate organizational willingness?

2. What characteristics of leadership do you think are essential to effective evaluation project management?

3. What constitutes a trusting relationship in an evaluation project? How do you know when there is trust between a client and an evaluator? What might indicate there is only tentative trust?

# 13

# THE EVALUATION FROM HELL

## When Evaluators and Clients Don't Quite Fit

Jacob Russ

## Marla Steinberg

*Marla Steinberg, PhD, CE, is an independent evaluation consultant and instructor who lives, works, and plays in Vancouver, British Columbia.*

One of the things that makes an evaluation "hum" for me is a good working relationship with my client. I don't expect us to become BFFs, but when every aspect of the evaluation seems to be conflict ridden, clearly something is not right. I am going to tell you a story about an evaluation that became known as "the evaluation from hell." It was hell because I found myself feeling very uncomfortable pretty much all of the time. Even though I have conducted about 50 evaluations and have over 25 years of experience as both an internal and external evaluator, this evaluation, which took place just a few years ago, really challenged me. I eventually came to the conclusion that I was a" bad fit" for this evaluation, but for a number of reasons, I had to continue with the project.

## ABOUT ME

I caught the evaluation bug about 30 years ago right after I finished my first evaluation course. I was introduced to a profession in which I saw I could make a living and pursue my passion for applied research. Under the guidance of an experienced evaluator, I began working as an external evaluation consultant. Over the years, I have been an internal evaluator for government and not-for-profit organizations and for the past six years or so, I returned to full-time evaluation consulting and added teaching to the mix. What is interesting to me is that I found myself in the evaluation from hell even though I have lots of experience in working with evaluation clients both as a consultant and as an internal evaluator.

## DESCRIPTION OF THE EVALUATION

As is typical for an external evaluation consultant, I was hired to develop and implement an evaluation for a new program that was being developed.[1] In this case, the program was being developed by a partnership of organizations. I was hired by the organization that was responsible for the evaluation of the program. From the beginning of the project, I recognized that I had two sets of evaluation stakeholders: my bosses (aka the people who hired me) and a steering committee composed of the partner organizations. Over the course of the program development phase, instead of developing a new program, a decision was made to adapt an existing program that one of the other partner organizations had already developed, implemented, and previously evaluated. This meant that one of the partners suddenly had more "skin in the game" (i.e., had more at stake) because their program was now the one being evaluated. It also meant that I now had three separate groups of stakeholders: the people who hired me, the steering committee members, and the developers of the repurposed program. In developing the evaluation plan, I was working in the way that I typically work: I was following my standard evaluation planning

---

[1] Kudos to the program for bringing in an evaluator at the program development stage!

practices of engaging all stakeholders, developing my deliverables for initial review by my bosses, then bringing the deliverables to the steering committee for review and final approval. The decision to repurpose the existing program also brought about a change in evaluation governance. I now had to co-develop the evaluation with the program developers and their own evaluation lead. Things started "heating up" almost immediately. Over a series of initial conversations, I realized that we had very different knowledge and understanding of evaluation.

## THE MISTAKE OR CHALLENGE

I was faced with a number of challenges in this multiyear project, all of which contributed to my feelings of being in hell.

First, I had to deal with the legacy of a previous evaluation that suffered from a poor methodology but was valued by the program developers. I did not want to reproduce what I felt was a poor evaluation design (including biased sampling and biased data collection tools), so I proposed different methods to what was previously done to answer the evaluation questions. I pointed out what was problematic with the previous work and what would be gained from what I was proposing. The program developers didn't always agree to my suggestions, which is common in any evaluation, but the level of scrutiny was much more intense than I was used to and the nature of the discussions was also different. While the merits and limitations of any particular method and sampling strategy are worthy of discussion, the decisions around evaluation design should be grounded by a consideration of what design will *best* answer the evaluation questions in the particular evaluation context. I started to question myself around rigour. Was I being too rigid in my thinking about evaluation quality and methodological rigour? In participatory stakeholder-driven evaluation, how far should the evaluator go in being responsive to stakeholders if it means jeopardizing the validity and quality of the evaluation? Did the program developers really want a bad evaluation, or was this just a bad fit between me and this client?

I also had to navigate my way through the stakeholders' understandings of evaluation concepts and divergent stakeholder evaluation needs. The program developers wanted a developmental evaluation (DE) and felt they had done DE in the past. They spoke about wanting to gather information that would help improve the program and were not interested in making summative judgements of whether or not the program was of value, should be continued, or adopted by the other organizations. The other stakeholders, however, wanted the evaluation to provide information to support program improvements but also wanted to collect information that would enable them to make decisions about whether to offer the program in their own organizations. Balancing different evaluation needs is not uncommon in evaluation. Designing an evaluation to address formative and summative needs is not difficult. The challenge here was in different understandings of evaluation, specifically the conditions under which DE is best suited. The DE literature offers very clear criteria for when DE is appropriate (see Patton, 2011), and in this context, the project did not meet the criteria. The program was pretty stable, and although the program was being adapted, the adaptations proposed were minor. The only truly complex element of the program that would have benefited from a DE was the identification of the longer-term outcomes, and this was not part of the scope of the evaluation. Although I was able to design the evaluation to provide both formative and summative information, I felt very uncomfortable calling it a DE. I had to think through how far I was willing to go in meeting stakeholder desires if it meant potentially negatively impacting my reputation.

Additional challenges were brought about through the new requirement that I work directly with the program developers' own evaluation-lead. It is not uncommon for external evaluators to find themselves working with (or for) program staff who have different views of evaluation or different levels of evaluation expertise. In an ideal scenario, these differences would surface during the evaluation hiring process where either the evaluator or client would assess the goodness of fit between the evaluator and the context. In less than ideal cases, like this one, these challenges crop up and can become a source of conflict throughout the evaluation process.

There were several other things that contributed to my feelings of discomfort, largely because they bumped up against my evaluation practices and integrity and I believed they could harm my reputation. I was not comfortable with the lack of evidence-base for the program or the absence of a coherent and explicit theory of change. I even found myself wondering if I had stumbled upon a situation where an independent external evaluation would be best rather than the participatory approach that I prefer and believe to be the best way to support evaluation relevance and use. Was I a bad evaluator because I could not deal with these challenges or, again, was this simply a bad fit?

Being uncomfortable in an evaluation is not necessarily bad; if explored and investigated, the discomfort can lead to useful insights and growth. Reflective practice is one of the Canadian Evaluation Competencies and in this evaluation, I spent a lot of time reflecting on my practice, my reactions to what was proposed and decided, my assumptions and principles, and, I must admit, my own feelings of competence (even though I have been doing evaluations for over 25 years!).

Jana Curll

I did a number of things to cope with my evaluation from hell. I wrote myself a sticky note and tacked it onto my computer screen to remind me to "Ask questions" whenever suggestions were made that I felt would jeopardize the quality of the evaluation. I thought that if I could better understand what the program developers wanted out of the evaluation, I could more easily understand their perspectives and perhaps suggest other ways of achieving their objectives while still providing a high-quality evaluation.

I spent some time researching stakeholder evaluation anxiety because I felt the amount of conflict was unusual and was likely caused by stakeholders' fears. (Remember I said the project had changed so that one of the partners now had more invested than the others?) I even posed a question to the EVALTALK forum on how to deal with evaluation anxiety. The suggestions I received were great, but I was already doing most of them (e.g., participatory evaluation planning and holding meaning-making sessions; see Donaldson, Gooler, & Scrivens, 2002).

I began to have regular venting/check-in sessions with an evaluation colleague and friend who was also involved in the project but in a peripheral way. These "evaluation therapy sessions," as I began to call them, allowed me to voice my frustrations in a safe space and check my reactions and suggestions with another skilled evaluator. My "evaluation therapist" confirmed my concerns and helped me brainstorm ways to move forward with integrity. This became my "out loud" reflective practice.

I considered and reconsidered leaving the project and letting the stakeholders know that their needs would likely be better met by someone who more closely shared their evaluation perspective or a more junior person whose job would involve simply implementing the evaluation as requested by the program developers. The problem was that if I quit, I would be letting down the people who had originally hired me, and they had hired me precisely for my expertise and approach. I fit with one group of stakeholders but not with those who had developed the program and were ultimately making the decisions about the evaluation.

In the end, I completed the evaluation from hell. It is funny to think that I was in hell not because of something I did but because of something I refused to do. I did the best I could working within the decisions that were made and continued to see my "evaluation therapist" throughout the project. I produced an evaluation report that was reviewed and revised amidst another round of heated discomfort. Was the report of value to any of the stakeholders? Other than enabling the organizations to fulfil their funding requirement of submitting an evaluation report, I don't know that it was used to support decision making; I rather doubt it. This is the rationale for utilization-focused evaluation: If you want stakeholders to use the evaluation report, you have to produce something of value to them, but when what is of value to stakeholders clashes with evaluator values, you have a bad fit.

## LESSONS LEARNED

- **Lack of evaluation fit can be pervasive.** The "lack of fit" between what the program developers wanted and my own evaluation practices and standards permeated every step of the evaluation process, including the following:

  - Focusing the evaluation
  - Selecting the evaluation approach

- Developing the data collection methods and tools
- Analyzing the data
- Interpreting the data
- Reporting

- **Reflective practice is valuable.** Asking questions, thinking through why I was uncomfortable, and sharing my reflections with a valued colleague helped me immensely with this evaluation. I strongly recommend that everyone find their own evaluation therapist—someone who is safe and able to offer an ear and advice. If you feel that the evaluation clients or program stakeholders are receptive, talk out loud with them about issues you see as they are emerging. In this way, you can engage in three types of reflective practices: reflecting on your own, reflecting with a colleague, and reflecting with program stakeholders and evaluation clients.

- **Assess evaluator and client fit.** The evaluation literature has much to offer evaluation commissioners in selecting an evaluator who is right for them, but little for evaluators themselves and even less for internal evaluators who are working with others from within their organizations (Community Tool Box, 2017). While our evaluator competencies and ethics instruct us to take on projects that match our technical and other skill sets, there is little guidance to help us assess other aspects of fit. Although I always believed that one-size-fits-all is a myth in clothing as well as evaluation, after my evaluation from hell, I would like to see more attention focused on evaluator and client fit. Wouldn't it be great if there was a site that evaluators could use to rate our clients? Here are some things to consider when deciding if an evaluation project is right for you or not:

  - Determine the decision-making structures or processes of the organization and meet with the decision-makers to try to assess compatibility with your own evaluation practices.

  - Research the organization's past evaluations and stakeholders' perceptions of them.

  - Meet with the key stakeholders and anyone else you will directly work with to uncover their knowledge of, and approaches to, evaluation. It is common to work with stakeholders with varying levels of knowledge and understanding of evaluation. Sometimes we are the evaluation experts when clients are not familiar with evaluation; other times we are hired because of our availability and we work with very knowledgeable clients who just don't have the time to do the evaluation. Both scenarios can work, as long as there is a good fit!

- **Consider an evaluability assessment.** External evaluators may find it very difficult to turn down evaluation opportunities or walk away in the middle of a project, but my evaluation from hell has taught me to really think through the fit with a new client. Remember, you are hiring a client as much as the client is hiring you. For internal evaluators, there is an added layer of complexity, as you may not be able to "turn down" a client or evaluation. If you are sensing lack of fit, consider doing an evaluability assessment to help determine if the program and staff are "ready" for evaluation and ready for you.

# REFLECTIVE QUESTIONS

1. What questions can evaluators ask prospective clients to assess fit?

2. What types of issues would make you consider terminating an evaluation project?

3. If you feel you must walk away from an evaluation before completing the work, what steps can you take to make the exit positive?

# REFERENCES

Community Tool Box. (2017). *Choosing evaluators.* Retrieved from http://ctb.ku.edu/en/table-of-contents/evaluate/evaluation/choose-evaluators/main

Donaldson, S. I., Gooler, L. E., & Scrivens, M. (2002). Strategies for managing evaluation anxiety: Toward a psychology of program evaluation. *American Journal of Evaluation, 23*(3), 261–273.

Patton, M. Q. (2011). *Developmental evaluation. Applying complexity concepts to enhance innovation and use.* New York, NY: Guilford Press.

# 14

# THE BEST LAID PLANS OF MICE AND EVALUATORS

## Dealing With Data Collection Surprises in the Field

Evan Noga

## Jan Noga

*Jan Noga, MEd, is the owner of Pathfinder Evaluation and Consulting, an independent evaluation consulting firm based in Cincinnati, Ohio.*

Even the best laid evaluation plans sometimes go awry. This is a story about setting a team of field-based data collectors loose in a school-based evaluation and the surprises that can creep up on you while collecting data in the field, including putting my foot in my own mouth in a big way.

## ABOUT ME

I am an accidental evaluator. In 1999, I was asked to join a university-based evaluation center to help with research design and writing. As I took on evaluation projects myself, I came to love the practical nature of evaluation, particularly its capacity building aspects—helping school-based programs innovate, improve, grow, and serve. I've been an evaluator ever since, primarily as an independent consultant. I'm also a systems geek and am one of the founders of the Systems in Evaluation Topical Interest Group of the American Evaluation Association.

The story I'm going to share occurred early in my career as an evaluator while directing my first team of field-based data collectors in a school-based evaluation. While painful to experience, I learned a critical lesson about the importance of misplaced assumptions in the context of training and preparing a team as well as interacting with program staff and stakeholders.

## DESCRIPTION OF THE EVALUATION

Soon after starting with my university's evaluation center, we were approached by a small city school district implementing a two-year pilot program to reduce student-teacher ratios in K-3 classrooms. The district was looking for an evaluation group that could help administrators and teachers learn more about how reduced class size influenced children's learning and classroom experiences prior to scaling the pilot to other elementary classrooms in the district.

I have to say, the district was a joy to work with. The two administrators supervising the project were very interested and engaged in designing a sound evaluation that would provide them with the information they needed. Prior to the first school year of the pilot, I met several times with my contacts at the district to identify their learning goals, articulate program logic, develop evaluation questions, and design a methodology. We settled on a quasi-experimental, group comparison design using a mixed methods approach to data collection that incorporated surveys of both parents and children, classroom observations, teacher interviews, student work sampling, and analysis of student achievement and assessment data administered by the district.

My design plate was certainly full. The overall purpose of the evaluation was to identify key factors affecting the classroom experiences of kindergarten and first-grade children during language arts instruction that could be attributed to reductions in class size. The reality of this meant developing instruments and data collection procedures to capture the following key elements:

- Teacher instructional strategies
- Frequency and nature of teacher-student interactions during language arts instruction
- Student engagement in learning
- Student and parent beliefs about school
- Teacher perceptions and beliefs
- Student outcomes in language arts

After a summer of development, the pilot was implemented in 12 kindergarten and first-grade classrooms located in six schools within the district. Evaluation activities started soon after, so at the start of the school year, I recruited and trained a six-person field-based team to conduct classroom observations, interview participating teachers, and survey students.

With so many types of data to collect, training and orientation for team members was essential. After developing the data collection instruments and protocols, I took team members through three half-day training sessions on the different types of data collection procedures we would be using. During training, we also practiced with the instruments and debriefed after each practice. Throughout the project, the team met every two weeks to share what was going on in the field and to raise any issues or questions that may have arisen.

Looking back, I can see that, while we spent valuable time practicing, I failed to provide my team with solid background on the methodological rationale for my choice of instruments, materials, or protocols. I also failed to cover the issue of what could, and more importantly could *not*, vary during data collection on site. I assumed that we were all on the same page in this regard, and, in doing so, did not provide my team with opportunities to raise concerns, ask questions, or indicate where there might be problems for them.

The student survey was particularly tricky. The quasi-experimental design required that the entire team be very consistent in using the instrument with the kids. We conducted the survey as an adapted sticker game with groups of no more than four or five children at a time. Children were given cards with a bingo-type grid on them, crayons, and sheets of neon-colored stickers. Everything was tested numerous times during development—the questions, the prompting instructions for helping students respond, even the choice of sticker colors. As an ex-preschool teacher, I was very much aware of the impact that color can have on young children; particular colors are strongly associated with gender typing. Over time, I had found that neon colors—light blue, green, and orange—were particularly successful with kids and were perceived as "happy" colors. I had also found that strong primaries—red, blue, yellow—were often perceived by children as "angry" or "grown-up" colors. Because we wanted the survey to be experienced as a game, we chose neon colors.

# THE MISTAKE OR CHALLENGE

We hit the field with enthusiasm. Bi-weekly team meetings went well with few problems being reported and no serious issues cropping up. I monitored data entry and observation instruments—no problems; everything was going smoothly. Clearly, I thought, the training and orientation sessions had prepared my team for everything. Little did I know that my happy bubble was soon to pop.

After a month of data collection, it came time for me to go out into the field to observe my team conducting observations and running surveys with the kids. Five of my team members were doing just fine with little to no difficulties cropping up as they worked with their classrooms. I scheduled time with the sixth team member, and that's when things went off the rails. This team member did not like neon colors—he told me later that the colors hurt his eyes. So, he took it upon himself to switch out the colors and use dark primaries—red, blue, and green—with the kids that he was surveying. He was on his third classroom of kids when I was finally able to get in to observe him. We're talking 90 kids that he had already surveyed. I let him finish that day, and then we went outside to talk. I asked him why he had veered from the protocol. Didn't he understand how important it was to stick to the protocol?

As we talked, it came out that he had vision and cognitive issues that were exacerbated by bright colors. He truly didn't see that this could be a problem, which was why he never mentioned his issues with neon colors in team meetings or in the trainings. He just assumed that he would be able to use any colors he wanted when he actually administered the surveys. He stated that he did not believe that color would really make that much of a difference. We decided to test this assumption and chose a dozen of the students he had just finished surveying, resurveying them using the neon colors. I could have cried—there was enough variance in their responses that we were going to have to survey the three classrooms all over again using neon stickers.

During a team meeting, we talked about what had happened. I explained that we were going to need to redo the three classrooms using neon stickers. Because the other five team members were still working their way through their classrooms and I was not going to force someone to use materials that caused physical discomfort, it fell on me to go back to the three classrooms and resurvey the kids. The new "neon" data was collected and compared to the original "dark primary" data—more than 75% of the kids responded differently. To determine whether it was color or the data collector that made the difference, I resurveyed a small number of children who had been surveyed by the other team members, again using neon colors. I found little to no variation from their original responses. Sticker color did indeed make a difference. I could not believe this mix-up was happening to me.

To add to the pile-on, while my team was busy surveying kids, I had been busy interviewing teachers. Fixing the sticker fiasco turned my scheduled three days a week in the district into five days a week for three weeks while I did double duty surveying kids and interviewing teachers. And that's when I doubled down on messing up.

I don't know if I was distracted, tired, or just frazzled from the sticker fiasco, but I really stepped in it while interviewing a team of two teachers. I interviewed each teacher individually. The first teacher I spoke with told me that she was not planning to return to the district during the second year of the project. In fact, she said that she had already found a position in another district. I then interviewed her partner and, as part of a follow-up to another question, I asked her whether she was going to get a new partner or teach solo during the second year of the pilot. She looked at me in shock, and it suddenly dawned on me that she had no idea that her partner wasn't coming back the next year. Needless to say, we wrapped up the interview soon after that question.

After the interview, the second teacher contacted her principal in tears. The principal had known that the first teacher was leaving but had not yet told the second teacher. The principal called district administration to complain, and I got called up on the carpet by the district about violating confidentiality of the interview situation. This was a very tense meeting, to say the least. At first, I had no idea what specific situation they were talking about. Once I had the details, I explained what had happened during the interview. In trying to make the interview situation more comfortable, I had let down my guard and crossed a line from inquiring to sharing. Thankfully, they were very understanding. But, let me tell you, I left that meeting feeling lower than low and kicking myself big time. It was a long,

Jana Curll

unhappy drive home for me. I seriously didn't know if I even wanted to continue with the project after that. Thankfully, I had a very good executive director who talked me down, helped me process what happened, and provided much-needed support during that very difficult time.

This goof was less easily resolved than the sticker issue, but we were able to come to closure. The administrator I was working with in the district met with the teacher and her principal and explained what she had learned during her meeting with me. I wrote a letter of apology to the teacher and received a very nice note back from her. It turned out that she and her partner had been having difficulties working as a team for quite some time. She had reacted as much out of shock at the news as out of a sense of betrayal by her partner. However, I knew that I was the source of that bad news and felt badly about that for some time.

That was a rough couple of months for me as a new evaluator, and that was only Year 1 of the evaluation! Fortunately, Year 2 went much smoother—no sticker fiascos, no interview disasters, and the only surprises were unexpected but intriguing outcomes that emerged from the data. The district was very happy with the information we provided and used it to guide them as they scaled up the pilot over the next few years.

# LESSONS LEARNED

- **The road to good intentions (and data collection) is mined with assumptions.** When it comes to training data collectors, just saying something doesn't make it so. For most of the team I was supervising, this was our first time working together. I made assumptions about the degree of mutual understanding and acceptance of protocols that didn't pan out. In particular, there were two critical stumbles. Although each team member had samples of the instruments and instructions for using them, these were provided in a very informal manner during the half-day orientation sessions. Instead, team members should have received instructional field guides containing evaluation goals and objectives, the evaluation questions, the data collection methodology and overall design, instruments and detailed protocols for their use, and a detailed project calendar. This guide should have been reviewed at the start of each training session and revisited on a regular basis during team meetings. Secondly, when data collection started, I should have met with each team member after their first day using each instrument to review the data collected, ensure that all protocols were being followed correctly, and explore any questions or issues that might have arisen. Although that may not have prevented the sticker fiasco, it would have certainly minimized the damage.

- **Evaluators often wear many hats in their professional activities. It is important that you're wearing the right hat when engaging with a program.** This evaluation was structured from the start as a fully external evaluation, as opposed to something more participatory or developmental. As a mixed methods evaluation with a large number of qualitative elements, it entailed large amounts of time in direct interaction with teachers, students, and principals at each school. It was not unusual for me to end up in the teachers' lounge during lunch or to have children in the classroom question me during my observations. At times over the two years of the project, I found my external evaluator hat slipping as the lines between me as external evaluator and me as colleague of the participants started to blur, resulting in that disastrous interview. In the service of putting the teacher, and perhaps myself, more at ease, I let my guard down and veered off track and off protocol—a painful but valuable lesson that I took to heart and now keep in mind whenever I am conducting an interview, be it structured, semi-structured, or wide open.

- **Evaluation is never a value-neutral activity.** Evaluations, and the programs we are evaluating, are often highly charged, with a number of systemic, professional, organizational, and interpersonal undercurrents at play. Our challenge is to acknowledge the value-laden and real-life nature of these undercurrents, to recognize and attend to what is happening both above and below the surface, to acknowledge that we are interacting with a situation in continual flux, and to be prepared to adapt and flex to emergent patterns that arise over the course of our work.

## REFLECTIVE QUESTIONS

1. What are useful ways to make sure that every member of an evaluation team understands exactly how to implement the evaluation protocol?

2. The evaluator in this story notes the importance of role identity as an external evaluator. What are your thoughts on role identity and the boundaries that might exist for an evaluator coming into a program? What skills are needed to successfully navigate these roles in a way that maximizes trust?

3. How would you interpret the statement, "Evaluation is never a value-neutral activity"? Do you agree or disagree with this premise?

# 15

# ARE YOU MY AMIGO, OR MY CHERO?

## The Importance of Cultural Competence in Data Collection and Evaluation

Venture Philanthropy Partners

### Isaac D. Castillo

*Isaac D. Castillo, MS, is the director of Outcomes, Assessment, and Learning at Venture Philanthropy Partners, and he has over 20 years of experience in evaluation, outcome measurement, and nonprofit management.*

As someone of Mexican descent who has received formal training as an evaluator, I am keenly aware of the need for culturally and linguistically appropriate evaluation practices. I have experienced first-hand the difficulties that service recipients face in accessing vital programming when they do not understand the language used or when existing practices are offensive or outside their cultural norms.

However, as a young evaluator, I was often part of the problem.

## ABOUT ME

As I was pursuing my master's degree in public policy at the University of Rochester, one of my professors mentioned to me that I would "make a good evaluator." Upon his recommendation, I entered the evaluation field 20 years ago and have focused on youth development evaluation and evaluation capacity building. I have worked as an external evaluation consultant and I have led internal evaluation departments at two separate direct service non-profit organizations. Currently, I am the in-house evaluation expert at a venture philanthropy organization. I often tell people that I am one of the few evaluators I know who can talk about the real-world challenges of conducting evaluation as a funder, as a grantee, and as a consultant, and I bring these three different but complementary views of evaluation to my work.

## DESCRIPTION OF THE EVALUATION

Early in my evaluation career, I was tasked with conducting data collection to determine why teenage gang members became involved in youth gangs, what it would take for them to exit the gang, and what it would take to prevent others from becoming involved in youth gangs.

In addition to developing the interview guides used in the qualitative data collection, I was also responsible for leading all of the on-site interviews in cities with large Latinx populations.

## THE MISTAKE OR CHALLENGE

I was born on the Texas-Mexico border, I am Latinx, and I had a good enough grasp of Spanish to confidently prepare the interview guides and conduct the interviews. I thought that I would be sensitive to all of the cultural and linguistic challenges to ensure an effective data collection process. Unfortunately, I had forgotten an important tenet of effective culturally competent evaluation. I had forgotten that cultures and languages are not monolithic. There are frequently differences in regional cultures or dialects that can lead even experienced evaluators into embarrassment, scorn, or the worst outcome of all: inaccurate data.

My assumption led to uncomfortable situations early on in the data collection process. For example, when first interacting with the gang members, I introduced myself and asked them to "Please sit down," to start the interview by saying "Sientate, por favor." What I did not know at the time is that a large portion of the gang members I was interviewing were born in El Salvador or were of Salvadoran descent, and the proper way to say it using Salvadoran Spanish would have been "Sentate, por favor."

Does one letter or one word make that much difference? In most cases it did not matter, as most of the interviewees understood what I was saying and just proceeded with the interview. But it caused several gang members to openly question my Spanish from the outset, which created an uncomfortable beginning to an interview about potentially sensitive subjects. Instead of creating an atmosphere where respondents felt comfortable and safe to answer questions honestly, I had started the interviews by sowing doubt and uncertainty.

The situation did not improve as I read the questions off my interview guides. I had tried to make the questions as casual and friendly as possible—after all, I was going to be talking not just to teenagers, but teenage gang members! I attempted to make the questions and content less "research-ey" and more conversational. But again, I had failed to acknowledge that all Spanish speakers are not monolithic and that regional variations in dialect can make a big difference.

My interview guides contained questions that asked the gang members to think of their "friends." In most dialects of Spanish, using *amigos* to ask about friends is accurate and proper. However, in the context of street slang and conversation, some Spanish-speaking gang members don't refer to their friends in this way. This is particularly true in Salvadoran communities, where the term *chero* is frequently used to refer to friends, especially in informal contexts.

Again, was this a huge mistake? No. But it did lead to enough quizzical looks and requests for clarification that I became concerned that I was not getting completely honest or accurate answers from some of the respondents. Fortunately, the data I received was consistent across all of the interviews and my concerns were eventually unfounded, but I feel I was lucky rather than smart in this instance.

In an ideal situation, these mistakes in question wording would have been identified and corrected after the first several interviews. However, the critical difference between *amigo* and *chero* did not arise until nearly 30 interviews had been conducted in total. Importantly, most of the Spanish language interviews took place in other cities and communities and I had not thought to test the wordings of the questions in multiple Spanish-speaking communities across several states.

In hindsight, I should have sent the interview questions ahead of time to my primary contacts in each state and community and asked them to provide feedback on the wordings. I should have also asked them to pay particular attention to language choice and wordings that may be more appropriate (or inappropriate) for each of their respective communities.

Perhaps my biggest (and most memorable) mistake occurred after I had completed an interview with a gang leader outside of a bakery. The gang leader and I had asked for privacy to complete the interview, but after we were done, the

Jana Curll

gang leader called over the rest of his gang to meet me. As I was meeting everyone, I glanced inside the bakery and noticed a Mexican pastry that I enjoyed as a child. I asked the gang leader if he would like to go inside and join me for a *concha*—which is what I grew up calling a round pastry that looks like a shell.

Everyone (except me) began to laugh hysterically.

The gang leader then let me in on the joke. He understood that I was asking about the *pan dulce* (sweet bread), but he informed me that in his dialect, *concha* was used as a vulgar reference to female genitalia. And he definitely did not want to join me in my quest for "genitalia." Fortunately, a situation that could have been offensive or degrading was viewed as an honest mistake. And it taught me a valuable lesson about how even casual references or language choices can be interpreted in many different ways.

## LESSONS LEARNED

These instances are memorable examples of how failing to think ahead about cultural and linguistic differences can negatively affect data collection and evaluation activities. While I can look back on these mistakes and laugh, I am also reminded of the important lessons learned that I carry with me to this day.

- **Translate with the local context in mind.** When translating materials or preparing for field work, it is important to get a detailed sense of who you will be collecting data from. This goes beyond just what language they speak, and should extend to what cultures and subgroups people represent and to whether there are specific topics or words that should be avoided. For example, when I started to first do work on youth gang issues in Washington, D.C., I was informed by multiple people that there are "no gangs in D.C." In D.C., they are called "crews," not "gangs"; any references to gangs will be met with a mix of laughter, confusion, or disdain.

- **Translate with the local population in mind.** When developing data collection tools (in any language, even if you are fluent in it), take the time to have individuals who are similar to future respondents review the language in the tools. This can help you identify wording or slang that may lead to confusion while also identifying and incorporating words that may be more appropriate for the research questions you are trying to address.

- **Be OK with your inevitable mistakes.** Recognize that no matter how much preparation you do, you will make mistakes in your data collection related to culture and language issues. If you do data collection long enough, I guarantee you will have your own *chero* or *concha* moment. The thing to remember is that your response in those situations is important: you must be respectful, you should learn why what you did is problematic so that you will not repeat the offense, and (if appropriate) don't forget to laugh at yourself.

## REFLECTIVE QUESTIONS

1. When constructing interview guides or survey questions, what can you do to ensure that the language used is appropriate for the population?

2. With respect to culturally and linguistically appropriate questions, is there a difference between items that will be read aloud versus those that will be read directly by potential respondents?

3. How would you handle a situation where you (or a colleague) used an inappropriate term or phrase with a research subject?

# 16

# OMG, WHY CAN'T WE GET THE DATA?

## A Lesson in Managing Evaluation Expectations

## Jennifer Bisgard and Mary Pat Selvaggio

*Jennifer Bisgard, MA Social Development, Johns Hopkins University, is a highly experienced evaluator, social change activist, and founder of Khulisa Management Services based in Johannesburg, South Africa, but working throughout Africa and the United States.*

*Mary Pat Selvaggio, MPH Public Health Nutrition, University of Minnesota, has evaluated health and other programs since the 1990s. A former USAID health officer, she leads Khulisa's health evaluation practice throughout Africa and elsewhere.*

How did we fail to see all the red flags? The evaluand told us they struggled to get their members to report financial data regularly. They also mentioned a database crash and that the donor wanted this to be a success story with substantial impact data, no matter what. But we merrily went on our way, ignoring these red flags for far too long.

## ABOUT US

We have been evaluators for over 20 years, running our evaluation company in Johannesburg, South Africa, since 1993. Both of us have master's degrees, Jennifer in social development and Mary Pat in public health. Our company, Khulisa Management Services, has approximately 30 employees and is known across Africa for our monitoring, evaluation, and data quality services.

## DESCRIPTION OF THE EVALUATION

The evaluation we would like to share initially seemed very straightforward, requiring a mixed methods approach, but also requiring that we validate their impact claims based on verifying routinely reported data.

Before we describe the evaluation, a note on the South African context. The period up to 1994, known as apartheid, was dehumanizing and incredibly restrictive for most of the population. *Apartheid* (an Afrikaans term meaning "apartness") was a rigid former policy of segregating and economically and politically suppressing the black population. This was a legal system from 1945 until the first democratic elections in 1994.

Apartheid meant that black South Africans were constrained in who they could love and where they could live, work, and be educated. They had no political voice. Appalling economic restrictions resulted in a tiny informal economy, with most black South Africans living in abject poverty without access to jobs or skills. Nelson Mandela's release in 1990 and the subsequent negotiated settlement leading to the 1994 demographic elections were watersheds in South Africa's history.

Based on the desire of large companies to "do the right thing," a group of corporations created a member-based nongovernmental organization (NGO) to promote black economic empowerment through support and linkages to black-owned small businesses, particularly women-owned businesses. An external donor funded this NGO to build the capacity of black small businesses to provide needed goods and services to its corporate members. The NGO aimed to create "matches" between their 27 corporate members and approximately 400 certified suppliers to facilitate greater procurement relationships between the two groups. The donor supported the NGO with a grant from 2012 to 2015.

In 2016, the donor commissioned us to evaluate the NGO's performance from 2012 to 2015.

# THE MISTAKE OR CHALLENGE

From the beginning, the evaluation began to go wrong. Instead of one joint inception meeting between us, the donor, and the evaluand (the NGO), separate meetings were held.

In the meeting with the donor, the project manager stressed that they needed quantitative data that could be linked to financial results such as "How much did the NGO's corporate members spend to buy goods or services from small black businesses?" and "How could this be shown as a success?" When we asked why the terms of reference did not include talking to the certified suppliers and only focused on talking to the NGO's corporate members, we were told that it would not be cost effective. The donor representative spoke at length about how his boss had high expectations for quantitative evidence of impact.

One reason (among others), he said, for the donor to commission the evaluation was that the NGO's routine monitoring had reported low numbers of "matches" between corporate members and certified suppliers. Thus, the terms of reference asked us, the evaluators, to verify the financial value of corporate member procurement (e.g., the amount the big corporates paid for goods or services from the small black businesses) from certified suppliers resulting from the NGO's capacity building. This involved requesting corporate procurement divisions to share spending data for the three-year period, namely, their overall procurement expenditure, the percentage of this expenditure that was with NGO-certified suppliers, and the percentage of this expenditure that was with other, noncertified suppliers. Although the NGO had regularly requested corporate members to routinely report this data, few actually provided this information. However, both the donor and the NGO assumed that corporate members would share this data more openly with an external evaluator even though they had been unwilling to share it with the NGO itself. This assumption was not just false—it was *incredibly* false.

A few days later, our introductory meeting with the NGO, which was originally scheduled for 90 minutes, extended instead to nearly 4 hours. The NGO, facing a financial crisis, was worried about the evaluation and anxious that their challenges be acknowledged. It was at this point we learned that their database, which contained the corporate members' routine reporting data, had crashed. They also aired their frustrations regarding those corporate members who didn't report regularly. Although we listened and heard this message, we neglected to interrogate it further.

We spent the next few weeks struggling to set up key informant interviews with corporate members, often running into a brick wall. Despite signing on as "corporate" members, buy-in to the NGO's program actually came from individual staff at the member companies (who gained prestige by sitting on the NGO board or hobnobbing with their counterparts for a good cause). When these individuals left the company or were promoted, there was no handover to another staff member, leaving the corporate member without a champion.

When we finally got around to analyzing the routine data, we realized, to our absolute horror, that the data was unbelievably incomplete, with most members only reporting erratically and insufficiently. We then realized the import of the "data crash"—the firewall, antivirus, and backup had completely failed, and the repair of the historic data set was grossly inadequate. Not only was there an abysmal lack of data to begin with, but what little that existed was lost in the crash.

Therefore, relying on the corporate members' cooperation to share their own historic procurement data became paramount to answering the evaluation questions. However, we continually ran into confidentiality concerns, indifference, and corporate staff who had never heard of the NGO. Many corporate members were unwilling to divulge the requested information, as they considered it too sensitive and confidential to share in an evaluation report that would end up in the public domain.

Things went wrong because the assumption that corporates would share their procurement and finance data was central to the verification portion of the evaluation, leaving us without an approach to attribute (or even contribute) towards the NGO's impact. Although the corporate members themselves governed the NGO, even the board could not convince its members to release the information to our evaluation team. Our team leader came from a corporate background, and we assumed that this would facilitate greater trust. But, we were wrong.

We overestimated the corporate members' commitment to the NGO and underestimated the sensitivity of the procurement and financial information. Although we signed confidentiality agreements, and cajoled and applied pressure, none of it was enough.

In the end, we succeeded in getting only partial data sets from six of ten corporate members. We used this limited procurement data as best we could to triangulate with the spotty routine reporting data that survived the crash.

At the end of the day (as they say in South Africa), we delivered an evaluation in accordance with the terms of reference. Although we were able to answer most evaluation questions, there wasn't sufficient data to document the impact. Backfilling the data was impossible, and there were many questions left about the magnitude and effects of procurement between the corporate members and certified suppliers. This lack of data was one of our major findings. But, we felt that we had disappointed both the donor and NGO given their expectations that the evaluation would sing their praises.

# LESSONS LEARNED

So now we are ultrasensitive to red flags! What would we do differently?

- **Recognize that evaluations aren't a remedy for backfilling deficiencies in routinely reported data.** If a program is unable to collect and report routine data, it is not always feasible or possible for an evaluation to fill the gap, even with a detailed verification process.

- **Better manage expectations around the evaluation.** Both the donor and the NGO thought that we could "rescue" the data to tell a better story about the NGO's impact. We realize now that our evaluation could never have met either of these expectations.

- **Schedule a joint inception meeting with all stakeholders to clarify and align expectations.** The separate meetings we held with the donor, the NGO, and the board meant that these stakeholders never heard each other's perspectives. In an ideal scenario, all stakeholders would meet with the evaluators and discuss each evaluation question and the associated data sources until reaching a consensus. Typically, this throws up potential issues; then the group can agree on alternative approaches and methodologies to mitigate risks.

- **Better understand the organizational context.** The lack of corporate champions was an important finding, but it also left us, the evaluators, without credible key informants.

- **Encourage clients and potential evaluands to consider doing evaluability assessments prior to commissioning an evaluation.** If we or the donor had conducted an evaluability assessment at the beginning of the evaluation, we would have realized that this extreme data gap could not be overcome by an external evaluation alone. In other cases, evaluability assessments can identify when the program hasn't progressed enough to be evaluated. This is a good idea and should probably be the first step in every evaluation, even if it seems straightforward!

**Evaluability Assessments**

- Is the evaluation feasible, given the theory of change and the potential evaluand's operational status and location? (Note: An evaluand is the thing being evaluated, be that a program, policy, organization, etc.)

- Is there sufficient routine and relevant data about the program, including appropriate management systems to provide it?

- Is there both utility and practicality in conducting the evaluation, given the views and availability of relevant stakeholders?

**References**

Davies, R. (2013). *Planning evaluability assessments: A synthesis of the literature with recommendations* (DFID Working Paper 40). London, UK: Department for International Development.

Rogers, P. (2013, January 2). *52 weeks of BetterEvaluation: Using evaluability assessment to improve terms of reference*. Retrieved from http://www.betterevaluation.org/en/blog/evaluability_assessment_to_improve_ToRs

# REFLECTIVE QUESTIONS

1. What could the donor have done before issuing the terms of reference for this evaluation? How might this have avoided the problems that occurred?

2. Could these actors' expectations ever be aligned? What role should an evaluator play in aligning these expectations?

3. What might have been an alternative data source for this evaluation?

# 17

# NO, ACTUALLY, THIS PROJECT HAS TO STOP NOW

## Learning When to Pull the Plug

Krishna Neale

## Karen Snyder

*Karen Snyder, PhD, MPH, has worked with NGOs, academia, government agencies, and philanthropic foundations with a focus on ending human trafficking, improving public health, and protecting the environment.*

M y radar did not go off when I learned the data analyst was unfamiliar with quantitative data. Nor did I see the red flags when we unexpectedly discovered private and confidential information in the data, or even when the total number of cases in the data set did not match the number of individuals surveyed. This is the story of how I learned to trust my instincts and take action when an evaluation is going off track.

## ABOUT ME

I am a doctoral-trained professional with over 20 years' experience improving policies and practices in anti-trafficking, health, and the environment. I have expertise in program planning, implementation and evaluation, qualitative and quantitative research, outreach, and communication in the nonprofit, government, philanthropic, and academic sectors. I get energy from helping demonstrate participatory approaches and meaningful change with diverse issues and populations, including gender and labour, sustainable agriculture, modern slavery and human trafficking, and global health.

I'll be transparent. This chapter is completely different from the first draft I submitted for this book. The first failure I described was a pithy, humorous, and all too familiar tale of a research project gone wrong. The failure was not the fault of any one person but rather a series of decisions by well-meaning staff in a worthy organization. But the story was not *my* failure as an evaluator and thus did not fit the theme of this book. As I prepared to withdraw my contribution, I reflected on my role as internal evaluator in this organization and realized that my failure was continuing a path of poor decisions, rather than saying, "No, actually, this project has to stop now!"

## DESCRIPTION OF THE EVALUATION

The specific project that led me to this failure insight is not especially important to this story. I took a position as the internal evaluator at a nonprofit organization. My responsibility was to lead the evaluative work of the organization— everything from building evidence about the theory of change, to managing external evaluators, to cleaning data from quarterly output indicator reports. As I eased into my new role, I reviewed orientation materials and spent some time with the person I replaced. It was exciting to be part of a dynamic organization that was serious about evidence and learning. In fact, I had been drawn to the organization by their clearly stated theory of change and well-developed monitoring and evaluation system. I was also impressed by how they valued reflection and learning. The content area was new to me, and I had not previously worked in an organization of this scale. I was nervous about getting up to speed on all of the work.

Despite my years of experience and the obvious interest that the organization had in hiring me, I was a poster child for "imposter syndrome"—when would they find out that I was really unequipped to be successful? But I leapt into my new position with both feet and a whirring brain. So much going on! So many details! So many meetings with new people! How would I ever feel in control?

One of my initial duties was to complete the analysis and reporting from a large household survey. The organization had developed and carried out the survey prior to my arrival as part of baseline data collection for an intervention. The qualitative and quantitative results were intended to provide a basis for comparison after 3 years. The data collection stage included external consultants, changes in staffing, several communities in a remote location, multiple languages, testing out new tablets and Open Data Kit, focus groups and surveys, and a rainy season that provided additional pressure to get the work done quickly.

Preliminary qualitative data analysis had been completed in the field by the time I got involved, but it was considered rudimentary and, in any case, needed translation to English. The quantitative data had been entered into Excel, and when I arrived at the organization, a master's-level student intern was cleaning the data and preparing to conduct the analysis using SPSS. My understanding was that things were under control and I would merely be providing oversight.

# THE MISTAKE OR CHALLENGE

I made the mistake of not trusting my experience and instincts. My radar did not go off when I learned that the intern had never used SPSS. Nor did I blink when I learned that they were using Google Translate to understand the survey questions and responses. Or when it turned out that private and confidential information was unexpectedly included in the data set. In this situation, there was a real possibility of repercussions if identities were revealed. And when we later discovered that the total number of cases in the data set did not match the number of individuals surveyed, I thought it reasonable to see if Statisticians Without Borders could help us out. They couldn't.[1]

Jana Curll

Despite these serious problems, there were external factors preventing me from abandoning the baseline report. The increased emphasis on evidence-based results in all aspects of development work meant that funders were becoming more discerning. The follow-up study required additional funding, so it was important to show that

---

[1] Shout out to Statisticians Without Borders! Awesome group of smart people who volunteer their time and statistical expertise to nonprofits.

the organization was capable of carrying out data collection through household surveys. There were also plans to extend this type of evaluation to other regions.

I desperately wanted all of the hard work and intention that had gone into this project to yield results, and I believed that with so much effort already invested, it must be possible. In other words, I did not give up.

As evaluators, we often struggle with simultaneously keeping track of all the details while staying true to the big picture. We all know that far too much research has been conducted "on" rather than "with" vulnerable populations. Everyone involved in this well-intentioned project was committed to participatory, gender-focused and human-rights-based approaches to research and evaluation. So we all viewed these challenges as the natural consequences of a real-world scenario and not the ideal described in methodology textbooks.

Pressing on, I was fully prepared to explain all of the limitations of the data collection and be cautious about making major conclusions from the results. I was also prepared to treat every setback as a "lesson learned" that would be addressed when doing the follow-up study.

It took over a year before I finally pulled the plug on the project and pronounced it "dead."

There was simply no way to carry out the analysis and establish baseline information for comparison. We were trying to turn straw into gold, but we did not have any magic to make it happen.

There was a lot of disappointment for me and my colleagues. It was really tough to make the call because I was afraid that others would be angry that I was dismissing their work. None of us wanted it to fail, and it was hard to acknowledge that despite all of the hard work and time that had gone into preparations and conducting the fieldwork, the data set was not going to be usable.

There was also, frankly, a small sense of relief. We could now redirect our time and resources to other monitoring and evaluation activities. Moving forward, I encouraged the organization to build on its strengths in program implementation and program evaluation and partner with academia and others to fill in gaps such as population research.

Nevertheless, it was really hard to give up on the data set. I even wrote a grant proposal later that included funding for a professional statistician to determine if there was anything that could be salvaged from the data. In the meantime, the intervention went on as planned, and we collected data on other monitoring and performance indicators. Although this new data does not allow for the pre- and post-comparison that had originally been planned, it has allowed a greater understanding of the intervention activities and outputs.

## LESSONS LEARNED

The data from this study is safely locked away in a password-protected database, waiting for a creative and experienced statistician to conduct a postmortem.

(Master's project, anyone?) But the more important outcome is my own personal growth from this failure. It wasn't until I reflected on my initial draft of this chapter that I realized that I could and should have trusted my own expertise and acted sooner.

- **Quit while you're ahead.** I should have ended this project after the first few months, recognizing that the poor data collection and initial data entry were not going to yield usable results. I now recognize that my knowledge and understanding of good data collection protocol was valid and that this project was not up to standards.

- **Use the American Evaluation Association (AEA) Guiding Principles.** I love the AEA Guiding Principles and use them as a reference when responding to grant or contract proposals. Reflecting on this incident, I think they can also be used to assess any evaluation experience—whether it is a new position as internal or external evaluator or taking on an existing project. Here are some questions to ask when embarking on a new-to-you project:

  - Systematic inquiry: Does this project adhere to rigorous technical standards for data collection and analysis? If not (Hello, Reality!), what can be done?

  - Competence: How will my skills and experience contribute to the project? How will I communicate with confidence?

  - Integrity: Can I stand by the results of this project, particularly when I was not responsible for the initial design and implementation?

  - Respect for people: Am I honoring or harming the perspectives and values of stakeholders with this project? Will their interests be served if the process is flawed and the results are inconclusive?

  - Responsibilities for general and public welfare: Are the time and resources invested in seeing this project to completion going to be justified by the results, if any?

- **Treat all projects as if you designed them yourself.** Next time, I will subject a new-to-me project to the rigor I would require if I designed the project myself. I will make sure of the following:

  - The evaluator and all stakeholders, including the clients and participants, are clear on the evaluation purpose and evaluation questions.

  - The feasibility of achieving this evaluation purpose and answering the evaluation questions is assessed.

  - Dummy tables for anticipated results are developed so that the data collection methods will yield results that help answer the evaluation questions.

- The evaluator and all stakeholders have a detailed understanding of how the data was collected.

- Data collection meets ethical requirements for privacy and confidentiality.

- **It is okay to make mistakes.** This is easier said than done. We are our own harshest critics, and we have to understand that taking the risk of making mistakes will help us be better evaluators.

- **Trust yourself!** Examine the situation, take different perspectives into account, and then make the choice that is right for you. Since this time, I have grown more comfortable with sharing my opinions, as well as directing and mentoring the work of others. I have steered the organization's monitoring and evaluation towards more rigorous, higher quality standards. Most importantly, I pay more attention to my instincts and ask a LOT more questions!

## REFLECTIVE QUESTIONS

1. Describe an experience when you decided to start over after substantial investment into something. What factors led you to make that decision?

2. What are some red flags that might indicate an evaluation is off track?

3. How would you react if someone else stopped a project in which you had already invested a lot of time and resources?

# 18

# MISSING IN ACTION

## How Assumptions, Language, History, and Soft Skills Influenced a Cross-Cultural Participatory Evaluation

## Susan Igras

*Susan Igras, MPH, is currently a research instructor and senior technical advisor at Georgetown University's Institute for Reproductive Health with evaluation experience that spans the African continent, Haiti, and India.*

I t was a beautiful Tuesday morning in a small district capital in East Africa and the core evaluation team was getting organized to begin the third day of data collection. Ministry of Health teammates present? Check. Project teammates present? Check. But where was the project manager, a key member of our participatory evaluation team? Day Three and once again MIA!

## ABOUT ME

My name is Susan Igras. When I took my first evaluation course as a Master of Public Health student, I found a subject area that resonated so deeply that I knew it would be part of my work wherever my professional path would lead me. I have been involved in global health for twenty-five years. I consider cross-cultural competency, belief in social equity, and fostering relevant programming as core principles that have guided my many experiences, not only as an international evaluation consultant but also as program director and technical advisor.

## DESCRIPTION OF THE EVALUATION

Some years ago, I led a mid-term process evaluation of a five-year, community-based family planning program in an East African country with a high population growth rate. Operated by an international nongovernmental organization (INGO) in three rural, very traditional regions of the country, the project used an ethnographic, incremental approach to increase acceptance and use of family planning services. In every village, project staff worked first with formal and informal village leaders to gain their permission and support to begin discussions of the issues with the larger community. An extension staff person then lived and worked in each village for three months to support social mobilization on the issues, establish a community resource person within the village, and create linkages with local family planning services. At the end of three months, he/she would move to a new village to begin the social mobilization and transfer process again. Over a five-year period, a significant proportion of villages in each region were to be reached.

I was living in Nairobi at the time, working as a regional advisor for health program planning and evaluation with the same INGO. Before I arrived in-country, I was briefed by the INGO's country program director. Monitoring data indicated strong increases in family planning method use in areas where the program was operating. There were, however, some serious implementation problems whose causes needed to be better understood to guide mid-course adjustments. Everyone (the government, the donor, and the INGO) was on board for a mid-term evaluation as this was a pilot intervention of great interest to the Ministry of Health, who wanted to potentially expand it to new districts. The mixed-method evaluation was designed to be participatory, and the INGO engaged a small core team of six persons. The team comprised three project and three Ministry of Health technical staff who would work together to design the evaluation and collect and compile data. In a sample of health facilities and their catchment areas, the core team would review project activity data, collect information from clinic registries to determine who was seeking family planning services, and hold interviews and discussions with ministry and community stakeholders. An expanded team would then join together to analyze and interpret the findings, before sharing results with staff, the Ministry of Health, and INGO senior management. I was looking forward to working in a fascinating country with new colleagues who had great technical health knowledge but limited knowledge and experience in evaluation. I was not only looking to build team members' evaluative thinking and skills and an appreciation of the discipline but also to learn from their practical health systems and community insights as we designed and implemented the evaluation together. I assumed that the core team was looking forward to the evaluation as well.

## THE MISTAKE OR CHALLENGE

The evaluation design phase was where I had my first inkling that something was amiss. Our initial evaluation team meeting was a good one. Most of the core team was present, although one key person, the INGO project manager, was unfortunately in the field preparing for the upcoming data collection. In a participatory fashion, I went through some basic questions and discussions about what evaluation is, why we engage in it, and what we want to get out of this mid-term evaluation. The meeting ended with defining roles and responsibilities for team members over the next two weeks of preparation and data collection. It was a good discussion and all appeared to be on board and ready to dig into the assignment.

The next day, the core team met again, this time to review and provide inputs into a matrix of evaluation questions and sub-questions that would guide instrument design for in-depth interviews, focus group discussions, and facility record reviews. Again, there were great questions and discussions arising from the participatory approach. As a team, we were starting to make new program evaluation connections and see how the evaluation would help us understand underlying issues that were challenging project implementation.

By the third meeting day, though, something had changed. Our task was to refine question guides. However, there were many more pointed discussions on specific questions in the guides, and people were noticeably uncomfortable with the exercise. As team leader, I thought I should acknowledge the attitude shift, so at one point I just stopped and asked, "What's wrong? What is everyone concerned about?" After a twenty-minute, somewhat circuitous discussion, it became apparent that people were deeply scared that there would be serious repercussions if the findings were not stellar. I had assumed that evaluation was a positive event, but from the team's perspective, past evaluations had often led to retribution and sanctions. Searching for a solution, I asked, "Should we call it something else?" The quiet response was "Yes, please." So, after more discussion, we renamed our evaluation a "mid-term review" and the team moved ahead.

What followed were long days and nights collecting data . . . and a bigger issue. We were on Day Three of seven planned days of data collection, moving from district to district, and coming together as a team each evening to review the day's work and discuss issues. The team was energized and excited about collecting data and gaining new understandings. But the Ministry of Health doctors on the team were not doing so well in the qualitative data collection arena. I had failed in assuming (too optimistically) the team's capacity to collect data. The doctors' interview notes looked like shorthand, much like writing prescriptions! Unfortunately, the doctors never did manage to write clearly over the remaining one and a half weeks of data collection, but the reality was that we could not adjust the team composition at this point. Even reorganizing team tasks was problematic given our small number. Although I was worried about the doctors' notes, I told myself that since other team members were doing high quality note-taking during interviews, we would still get sufficient insights.

But my bigger issue was the project manager, who seemed to be trying to sabotage our data collection by mismanaging daily logistics, not doing her data collection tasks, and not working on team tasks in the evenings ostensibly because she had to organize things for the next day. Her physical and mental detachment was

apparent to the entire team, although we all remained silent on the issue during our evening debrief meetings. But I was confused. Why was she continually MIA? Wouldn't she want to find out more about the evaluation's progress? My third incorrect assumption was that she would naturally want to learn about the program design and performance issues in order to address them, but it appeared I was wrong.

The team managed as best it could, but after three days of tacit disruption and one inconclusive discussion initiated by me with the project manager about what was going on, I decided I had to call her supervisor. This was not an easy decision for me to make and I felt conflicted. As an internal evaluator of an INGO, I was often asked by senior management to give my opinion of the staff people I worked with. I always answered carefully, aware of my power and privilege and the possible consequences of being too frank. Soon thereafter, the project manager left the evaluation team and only rejoined us during later dissemination events. The team never spoke about why she might have wanted to sabotage the evaluation process. With her departure, though, I think people felt relieved and we functioned more strongly as a team as a result.

I did not have an issue with speaking to the project manager's supervisor; the evaluation would have been threatened if I had remained silent. As team leader, though, I still wonder if I should have discussed her performance with the core evaluation team, using the discussion as an evaluation learning moment. Would such a discussion have been culturally appropriate, or was the absence of discussion the culturally appropriate response? Would I have transgressed some hierarchical boundary of discussing personnel issues within an organization or with ministry representatives, diminishing my credibility in the process? The project manager left the INGO a few months after the evaluation. To this day, I wonder how much I was responsible for her departure and if there was a way I could have managed this differently.

In the end, our multi-organizational and cross-cultural team had enough data to do a comprehensive analysis of the project implementation process, pinpoint conceptual gaps and process issues, and identify solutions. Our participatory evaluation perspective as a group of project insiders and outsiders, shored by defensible findings, led to actionable solutions. The project consequently made adjustments, and we all felt happy that our recommendations were acted upon.

# LESSONS LEARNED

- **Check your assumptions throughout the evaluation process.** I made a number of erroneous assumptions during this evaluation. I failed to sufficiently acknowledge cultural context when beginning the evaluation, incorrectly assumed that all team members would have the capacity to produce useful interview data, and only in retrospect understood that a project manager might prefer to sabotage an evaluation rather than publicly acknowledge her project's performance issues. It is easy to forget that others in an evaluation process have different backgrounds and motivations; it is important to continually reflect whether your assumptions are correct.

- **History matters.** The widely felt evaluation fears held by the team had, I believe, historical roots. Punitive, feudalistic societal structures had only been eliminated one generation earlier, and all team members, including the project manager, were fearful. Each time I go to a new country, I now do some preliminary learning about the political and social history to help ground the evaluation context. This is an important element for gaining cultural competency.

- **Language matters.** What we call evaluation in one setting may require a different name in another. It is irrelevant to the cause when the process remains the same. And you can still build evaluation capacity without calling it evaluation.

- **Soft skills are critical for evaluation success.** This is not something that is easily taught. Being open and intuitive, understanding negotiation, having skills to manage team dynamics, and knowing when to be direct and when to act indirectly, all while maintaining evaluation standards, often come simply from experience. I learn something new about engaging with people (or relearn something old) almost every time I undertake an evaluation. The point is to be conscious of the tools in your soft skills toolbox and when and how to execute them.

- **Leading a participatory evaluation demands flexibility and practicality.** Participatory approaches to evaluation have important roles to play in building stakeholder capacity and appreciation of data and evaluation processes. But you do not often get to choose your teammates and, as this story demonstrates, anything can happen. How this affects the evaluation process will vary. Depending on the team's skill set, you may need to adjust roles and responsibilities during the design, data collection, and analysis phases. As you learn about the team, try to find the best fit of tasks for each skill set, and be flexible with your expectations.

- **Consider organizational culture carefully if engaging management in evaluation problem solving.** The role of cross-cultural evaluator almost always takes you into the world of organizational politics intermingled with cultural sensitivity, with few guideposts. As an outsider, it is a delicate decision about when and how to approach senior management about one of their staff. As you start an evaluation, it is always good to socialize and develop casual relationships with people not directly engaged in the evaluation. You might gather information useful for the evaluation. But it also opens the possibility of a later check-in with a friendly person who can help you understand organizational sensitivities before approaching management about a staff person or other organizational issue inhibiting a quality evaluation.

## REFLECTIVE QUESTIONS

1. What could you do as a cross-cultural evaluator to develop your own cross-cultural competencies both prior to an assignment and once in-country?

2. Given this was a participatory evaluation that engaged project and ministry teammates with differing skills and potential, and different political motivations, what safeguards could you put into place to ensure the quality

of the evaluation at different stages—from planning and design, to data collection, data analysis, and dissemination?

3. Soft skills, besides teamwork, are rarely taught in graduate school, but they can make or break an evaluation process. In addition to gaining experience on the job, how might you work to deepen your range of soft skills so you can effectively employ them during an evaluation?

# 19

# "THIS IS HIGHLY ILLOGICAL"

## How a Spock Evaluator Learns That Context and Mixed Methods Are Everything

Mélissa Proulx

## Benoît Gauthier

*Benoît Gauthier, CE, MA, MPA, CMC, AdmA, is a professional evaluator trained in political science, quantitative methods, and public administration who has spent the last three decades developing knowledge in support of better decision making.*

Three decades ago, I was taught, on the job and as part of the organizational culture I worked in, that evaluation was about the determination of the incremental impact of government programs. Like Spock from the old television series *Star Trek*, in my evaluation universe, the logic model reigned—you know, a program depiction that is entirely centered on the program with no recognition of environmental factors or their effect on program logic. This is before theories of change became the new rage. This worked for me for several years, but eventually this narrow view of evaluation got me into a difficult situation. Some twenty years into my stint as an evaluator, I completely changed my take on evaluation. Here is how it happened.

## ABOUT ME

I am a professional evaluator and have practised evaluation since 1984. As a private consultant I have been called upon to conduct a number of other types of studies involving social research methods; however, evaluation has always been my first professional interest. I am a strong advocate of collective action in professional associations. I was president of the Canadian Evaluation Society in 2014–2016, treasurer and vice president of the International Organization for Cooperation in Evaluation and a member of the EvalPartners Management Group in 2016–2019, and vice president of the *Réseau francophone de l'évaluation* (Francophone Evaluation Network) in 2017–2019.

I became an evaluator without really knowing it. At the beginning of my work life, before I had regular employment, I was told by an acquaintance that there was an opening in the public service for an "evaluator." I was invited to a job interview and prepared by quickly reading up on the Government of Canada guidelines for evaluation. I was lucky to be chosen for this job, which became a career despite no previous planning. At that time, there was no university program in evaluation in Canada: every evaluator was first an economist, a sociologist, a psychologist, or a political scientist (like me). My training and my interest were in social science methodology—quantitative analysis, really. This was well suited to my understanding of evaluation as the application of social science to estimating program impacts.

Boy, was that a restricted view!

## DESCRIPTION OF THE EVALUATION

Years ago, I was brought in as an external evaluator to lead an evaluation of a program that offered monetary benefits to successful individuals. The program was not complicated. Applicants were pre-selected by institutional partners, so they were all suitable for the benefits. Then, the organization in charge of the program identified who, among those pre-selected individuals, would receive the top tier of benefits, who would receive the middle tier, and who would not receive benefits. This selection was based on a paper review and driven mostly by a single quantitative indicator of past behaviour. Because the program had a fairly long history and was entrenched in a strong corporate and disciplinary culture, there was solid consensus around the logic of the program and its expected outcomes.

Considering this, I was quite at ease with the internal evaluation team's selection of an approach that would comprise qualitative and quantitative data gathering and analysis. As a consequence of my training (and some say of my Spock-ish personality), I was predisposed to the quantitative data, in particular, the survey data that we could gather from thousands of program applicants. I also gravitated to the use of a quasi-experimental design with one treatment group (high dosage with the top tier) and two control groups (low dosage with the middle tier and no dosage with those not selected for benefits).

We could afford to develop a very complete measurement model because there was ample literature on the type of benefit that was provided by the program and the expected results, as well as the circumstances associated with success, such as the socioeconomic status of the family. We went on to develop a very long questionnaire to measure all expected results and to cover (and later statistically control for) all the covariates identified in the literature. This was quite important to me as a quantitative analyst because there was a real risk that the selection process used as part of the management of the program would systematically bias the outcomes in favour of a conclusion of program success.

Once the data were all in, we started to compile results. That meant synthesizing qualitative evidence (essentially, interviews with stakeholders and program recipients) and massaging a very large database of survey results. This involved building large and sophisticated multivariate models of incremental program effects that took into consideration all the relevant covariates.

In the end, after careful verification of the data processing, the observations from the quantitative analyses were inescapable: the program's top tier of benefits made essentially no difference in expected outcomes over and above the middle tier, and the middle tier made essentially no difference over and above the absence of benefits. The qualitative evidence did not lead to the same conclusion, but then again, isn't it "always" the case that people tend to drastically overstate the consequences of benefits they received? That would not be a first, would it?

Once all the evidence was factored in, I concluded that this long-standing program, which had the unwavering support of management, produced nothing and had no reason for being. At least, that's where the quantitative evidence logically led me.

## THE MISTAKE OR CHALLENGE

Throughout the evaluation, the internal evaluation manager had expressed concerns that I was not understanding the program correctly. But he was not very explicit in his comments. Perhaps his discomfort was intuitive and he lacked the

Jana Curll

ability to articulate it well to me, the same ability that I would soon discover I was missing as well. I replied (several times) that the evaluation design and analyses were absolutely aligned with the logic model (as I said earlier, this took place before theories of change became popular in my area of the world). Therefore, how could I go wrong? Anything else was, as Spock would say, "highly illogical."

Well, I could go wrong. Very wrong in fact. I did not take *context* into consideration. As I learned some time after the completion of the evaluation, it turns out that the three segments of beneficiaries (high dosage, low dosage, no dosage) had each evolved in very different contexts but were integral parts of the same system. In the first segment, all applicants were considered of significant value by the pre-selecting organization and were provided special treatment via the top tier of benefits. In the second segment, recipients were provided a lower dosage of benefits but were still immersed in the same overall success framework as the first segment. In the third segment (no dosage), applicants did not receive program benefits, but, unknown to me, they were always nonetheless supported by the institutional partners that made the pre-selection. Segment three was left on its own as relates to benefits from the program being evaluated, but that did not mean without other support from the institutional partners, as I later discovered. I failed to perceive the relative position of these segments in the same system and interacting with each other; I failed to situate the program in its larger context. In particular, I failed to acknowledge and to factor in that the program was simply one mechanism to support the applicants among a battery of mechanisms that were managed by other agencies, within the same overall system. Without the program, the system in which the applicants revolved would pick up the slack but only to the extent that the financial resources of the institutional partners would allow. The program in question was one component in a larger system, but I evaluated it with blinders on, not assessing how the existence or the demise of the program would affect the entire system of support.

I felt on absolutely firm ground with the quantitative evidence from my quasi-experimental design, my elaborate measurement models, and my sophisticated multivariate analysis. This program did not work. However, the reaction from the program managers was less than kind. In their view, the evaluation results made no sense, because they knew of so many instances where the program made a difference. But they were not equipped to criticize the intricate methodological design that I had put to the task, and I did not help them translate their concerns in order to better interpret the findings. In their official response to the evaluation, program managers dismissed the results and argued not for a continuation of the program but, in fact, a reinforcement of it. I thought that I failed because I had not convinced them of the error of their ways. In fact I failed because I had not properly understood the dynamics of the program and the context in which it operated.

## LESSONS LEARNED

After carefully reflecting on this experience, I took away several important lessons learned.

- **Listen, listen, listen.** I could have avoided my error by listening more intently to the program and evaluation stakeholders. They knew that my approach was narrow-minded, but they were unable to use my jargon to explain why. And I was unable to understand their position because I was confined to my quantitative and mechanistic view of the world. As the evaluator, I was responsible for considering the views of all relevant stakeholders and for building their own understanding of their program logic into my evaluation. Evaluators must consider such input as hypotheses, but it is crucial not to dismiss it as ill-informed.

- **Recognize diversity.** I could also have avoided this mistake by not treating the beneficiaries as a monolithic block. I failed to acknowledge the context of the program and its implementation, and I limited my understanding to the established program logic. The evaluator is responsible for ensuring that the complexity of the program is accounted for.

- **Logic models are useful but should not limit our thinking.** I now recognize that our beloved logic model is limited in scope and use. Logic models constitute one of the key tools in evaluation practice. Constructing them is an opportunity to understand and make explicit how the program is supposed to work and what outcomes are expected. But logic models are program-centric and put the evaluator at risk of remaining program-centered, too. Instead, programs are one component of a larger systemic environment; they contribute to it and they are influenced by it. Theories of change are much more adept than logic models at identifying contextual factors and at warning the evaluator about the complexity of the system in which the program takes place. Collectively, our profession still has work to do to better define these tools and to integrate them into a global understanding of program dynamics. I now advocate for the use of what a colleague and I call "causal models." Where logic models and theories of changes are centered on the program and its contribution to the outcomes, causal models are centered on the outcomes and depict the key chains of independent variables that affect these outcomes. Causal models clarify that the program is far from being alone in the systems dynamic of the social or economic issue at play.

- **Be a realist.** This project led me to question my overall approach to evaluation and to give much more weight to qualitative and contextual evidence. In short, my "highly logical" Spock has now become a more human Captain Kirk. I still believe that good quantitative evidence tells a credible story, but I am warming up to the importance of people, context, and mechanisms that is highlighted in the realist evaluation approach. Realist evaluation focuses on "what works for whom, in what contexts, in what respects, and how." It views a program intervention as the selection of one mechanism to effect a change in instances where several other mechanisms could have been used. It also recognizes the importance of context and the possibility that different types of beneficiaries may react differently to the change mechanism used.[1]

- **Communicate, communicate, communicate.** It is clear that I could have paid more attention to communicating with the internal evaluation manager, working with him to better articulate his discomfort. This would have helped me better recognize the complexity of the program environment. In evaluation, context is everything, but communication is also key for clarifying this context. The evaluator is responsible for ensuring that communication takes place among all parties that share a similar level of power—as opposed to the situation I just described where the evaluator-as-technician imposes his views on others who may not be equipped to argue. The evaluator may be in a position of power because he relies on his methods and established practices, but, as this example shows, this position of power may not produce the best evaluative outcome for everyone.

- **Work on your own imperfections.** Finally, I realize that I need to perpetually evolve as an evaluator and that what I believe is quality evaluation today may well not cut it tomorrow. Self-reflection is sometimes difficult: most people prefer to avoid the cognitive dissonance that sometimes results. But evaluators must continually question their own practice by considering the benefits of alternative evaluation approaches, reading up on new ideas penetrating the field, taking part in discussions with other evaluation professionals, and taking time to observe their own evaluation successes and failures.

---

[1] Read more at Westhorp, G., Prins, E., Kusters, C., Hultink, M., Guijt, I., & Brouwers, J. (2011, May). *Realist evaluation: An overview. Report from an expert seminar with Dr. Gill Westhorp.* Wageningen, Netherlands: Wageningen University & Research Centre, Centre for Development Innovation. Retrieved from http://edepot.wur.nl/173918

# REFLECTIVE QUESTIONS

1. How would you approach a situation where the program managers and stakeholders think that you, the evaluator, have misunderstood the program results?

2. What could you do to better help stakeholders articulate their concerns about a program or evaluation?

3. The journey through a career in evaluation is heavily influenced by one's enculturation into the profession. How can you avoid becoming rigid in your practice and ensure that you remain professionally agile?

# 20

# THE RIPPLE THAT BECAME A SPLASH

## The Importance of Context and Why I Now Do Data Parties

Diana Tindall

*Diana Tindall, MPA, CE, is an independent evaluator who conducts research on program and organizational performance.*

fell in love with evaluation as a student. What could be better than a career contributing to highly rational, research-based solutions for sticky social problems? Well, it turns out it's a bit more complicated than I expected. Especially when the news is bad.

## ABOUT ME

I'm a mixed-up evaluator. After training to be an internal evaluator, I've been an external evaluator for more than twenty-five years. I've worked as an evaluation co-op student, as an evaluation consultant with a large national research company, and as an independent evaluator. I've worked on federal, provincial, and not-for-profit sector projects. I've done mixed methods research on education, labour market, community, health promotion, and industry development programs. It's been a muddled journey.

The situation I'm about to relate highlights the importance of context in evaluation. It also calls attention to the benefits of involving stakeholders in interpreting findings and emerging issues. And it emphasizes the value of both of these, particularly when there is "bad news."

## DESCRIPTION OF THE EVALUATION

Some years ago, I was working on the evaluation of a multi-site program with a central program management team. The central management team worked in the regional capital, and more than thirty sites were spread out across the region.

Each year the program would ask for proposals and approve and fund projects at sites—sometimes the same sites and sometimes new sites, depending on the proposals. It would also monitor how the projects were going and ask for wrap-up reports.

The evaluation was to look at both implementation and outcome evaluation questions. An evaluation working group steered the evaluation. This group comprised central management staff, their director, and the organization's internal evaluation staff.

The organization's internal evaluation staff created the evaluation plan. They hired our external evaluation team to implement it over three months. I led the evaluation team. The evaluation used multiple lines of evidence including a document/data review, surveys, interviews, and focus groups.

## THE MISTAKE OR CHALLENGE

During our data collection, we learned that one of the site staffs' concerns and suggested improvements was the need for more communication with the central management team. At the time of the evaluation, existing communication took place in two ways. Central management staff would try to check in with each site for an interim mid-cycle update. They would also communicate on an as-needed basis to problem solve. They checked in with sites by phone, by email, or, occasionally, in person. However, site staff considered this to be insufficient. They wanted more ongoing communication, perhaps bi-weekly or monthly rather than only mid-cycle. Site staff also wanted better communication around a wider range of topics. They wanted to talk about not just whether they were meeting their project objectives but how they were meeting them, what smaller challenges they faced, and how to address them. They were also interested in learning what other sites were doing when faced with similar issues. Site staff were explicit and consistent about their communication concerns in their survey, interview, and focus group remarks.

We drew on these comments to draft a conclusion about gaps in communication. We wrote a related recommendation to increase communication and included them in the draft evaluation report. Despite the evaluation's mostly positive findings, this negative one was not well received by the central management team. If the conclusion around communication had been positive, it would hardly

have made a ripple. But a negative conclusion always garners more interest, doesn't it? And this one created quite a splash.

We presented our findings at a meeting with the evaluation working group. They had received our draft report before the meeting, and there was a definite chill in the room when we arrived. Our presentation went quickly. And then the clashes began. I anticipated some discussion around the conclusions. But I didn't anticipate the level of defensiveness and negativity on this particu-

Jana Curll

lar one. To be honest, at times the splash felt like a tidal wave. I had hoped for a discussion around "reasons why" and "actionable options." Instead I got outright refusal to accept that there was any issue with communication at all.

The central management team clearly felt that the existing level of communication was more than enough to meet the program's needs. In their opinion, there was sufficient communication for them to confirm that the sites were on track. If sites weren't, they believed they were able to work with them to get back on track. In addition, they felt overextended with the amount of work they were already doing, given the program's limited resources. They simply didn't have time for more ongoing communication with sites. In short, they were very upset.

I left the meeting with a hollow feeling in the pit of my stomach and a sense that we had failed. It seemed like all our hard work and research was being discounted because of this one finding. I started to second guess myself. Could we have got it wrong? How could we have mistaken a splash for a ripple? I went over and over our evidence to be sure that we had the research to prove it. I created possible alternative explanations, which circled around in my mind. I slept very little that night.

Soon after, we discussed our next steps with both the central management team and the organization's internal evaluation staff. With the central management team, we discussed the basis and context for our conclusion as well as feasible actions. We told them of the site staffs' concerns and suggested improvements. We talked about the kinds of communication gaps and changes site staff hoped to see. In response, the central management team spoke of their own constraints and priorities. They talked about their lack of time and resources. They discussed how time consuming the communications they were already doing were, especially given the number of sites they worked with. With the organization's internal evaluation staff, we discussed various options for addressing the contentious conclusion and recommendation. We could leave them as they were, we could remove them, or we could modify them. All were possible actions.

We reviewed the new contextual information emerging from our discussions with both groups. We went back to our raw data. And we discussed what we could or could not substantiate—as well as what that meant for our options.

In the end, we modified the conclusion to reflect that it was a concern presented by sites. We kept the findings as they were and added more on the sources of the evidence—the survey, interview, and focus group responses that formed the basis for our conclusion.

We added more contextual information on the existing level of communication from the central management team and their staffing and budget constraints. We chose not to go into detail on the program's resourcing priorities. But we noted that resourcing levels placed limitations on the extent to which the central management team could increase the amount of time spent on communication.

We also revised the recommendation to suggest possible low resource actions that could be taken to meet site needs rather than those of the program as a whole. These included introductions between sites so they could share more with each other, a central "discussion board," and a newsletter for communicating about common interests.

By the end, we had a report that everyone accepted. The central management team still wasn't thrilled with the negative news. But they accepted the evidence from the site staff data. And they were more open to options for trying to increase the amount of communication taking place. As the evaluators, we felt good knowing that the conclusion and recommendation accurately reflected the evidence. And I felt we'd finally found a workable solution.

# LESSONS LEARNED

- **Acknowledge the importance of context.** We learned the importance of returning to our sources to gather contextual information around emerging issues. We had multiple lines of evidence for concluding a lack of communication, including site staff views. However, we did not sufficiently incorporate the context within which the central management team operated and their perspective before we drafted the final report. In particular, we didn't ask for their views on why the communication levels were as they were. Although we had met with the central management team while planning the evaluation and interviewed them as stakeholders, they did not raise communication as a particular concern during these discussions. And once we'd heard from the site staff, we didn't return to the central management staff to discuss these views. As a result, the central management team initially discounted the evidence associated with this finding and considered it threatening. We didn't have their buy-in for the issue as a relevant priority or for the recommendation made.

- **Hold a data party.** Moving forward, I also learned the importance of involving the program team in analysing the preliminary findings. A data party is a participatory data analysis session with stakeholders, facilitated by the evaluator. The stakeholders invited may be central management staff, site staff, participants, board members, external advisors, or others involved with the program. It provides an opportunity for stakeholders to work with the evaluation data and each other to discuss the findings. The facilitator can use different techniques to moderate the discussion and manage the group's dynamics. But the overarching goal is to get a better understanding of the findings through involving stakeholders in its interpretation. I now regularly hold data parties to accomplish the following:

  - Provide an opportunity to discuss positive and negative findings in a non-threatening manner.

  - Reveal context—information on priorities, facilitators, limitations, and previous practices—pertinent to interpreting the findings, understanding emerging issues, and drawing conclusions.

  - Identify priorities, confirm relevance, and develop actionable options (with buy-in) for recommendations while ensuring they are consistent with and supported by the evaluation's evidence.

Together, these lessons can help evaluators avoid getting soaked by an unanticipated splash.

# REFLECTIVE QUESTIONS

1.  How can evaluators incorporate context into their conclusions and recommendations if it doesn't come up during the evaluation itself, for example, if new issues emerge after data collection is completed?

2.  What mechanisms can evaluators use to link evidence to specific conclusions? How can we be explicit about the basis for conclusions and the recommendations associated with them?

3.  What steps can evaluators take to improve stakeholder buy-in for their conclusions and recommendations? What actions can they take to increase stakeholder understanding of evaluation findings and possible actions?

# 21

# THE VOLDEMORT EVALUATION

## How I Learned to Survive Organizational Dysfunction, Confusion, and Distrust

## Lisa O'Reilly

*Lisa O'Reilly, MPA, CE, is an evaluator with diverse experience: working domestically, internationally, internally, and externally.*

Of the four of us on the evaluation team, one quit the first day of the field visit, one has completely erased the evaluation from her memory, and one calls it "Voldemort" because she refuses to say its name.

## ABOUT ME

My name is Lisa O'Reilly. I started in evaluation in 2002 and have worked as both an internal and an external evaluator in Canada and abroad. The situation I'm about to relate was from the first half of my professional career, when I had just started working as an independent evaluator. It was a total disaster and is not on my résumé.

## DESCRIPTION OF THE EVALUATION

My client was an international development organization based in North America that focused on farming techniques. They developed tools and guides for staff, who then provided training to local farm co-ops across multiple countries. This was a formative evaluation, focused on improving the program in one country, which would inform operations in other countries.

The Evaluation Steering Committee included the organization's new in-house evaluator at headquarters, a new regional program head, an in-country program lead, and two field staff. They were spread across five cities in three countries, none where I was based. Communication was primarily asynchronous, with a few tele-conferences for key discussion points. The plan was to work collaboratively with the Steering Committee and staff to do the organization's first ever evaluation.

This was one of the first "big" evaluations that I'd won competitively with me as the lead. Although I had done evaluations before with smaller organizations or as part of a team, I was aware of my relative inexperience and tried to pull together a good team for this project. There were four of us on the evaluation team: me, two senior advisors who I had known for years (one who specialised in agriculture and one who was very experienced internationally), and a local colleague. The local colleague was a friend of a friend already based in one of the organization's project communities who we found through our professional network. All in all, we had over seventy years of experience, subject matter expertise, context, and local language skills. To add to this, the organization provided a second evaluator, newly hired to their regional office in a neighbouring country, who would join our team for the field research, giving us a second native speaker in the field. So far, so good.

## THE MISTAKE OR CHALLENGE

In retrospect, the first kick-off teleconference with the Steering Committee had red flags that I missed. The in-house evaluator was clearly nervous, the second evaluator from a neighbouring country who had planned to join me in the field announced that she couldn't get an entry visa and said nothing more, her boss (the regional program head) was distractingly enthusiastic about sharing the evaluation results with potential funders, the in-country program lead was available for only a brief period during the call, and the two field staff didn't participate. The agenda had been to review the draft evaluation plan that we proposed. This was abandoned. We agreed that my team and I would begin a document review, and the rest of the evaluation plan would be discussed asynchronously. However, there was barely any communication during the crucial evaluation design phase. Time zone differences and limited access to electricity and/or internet were blamed, although I suspect this was not the case.

I was scheduled to travel overseas to meet my local colleague to begin the field research, but I had hesitations because of the lack of progress on the evaluation plan. I couldn't figure out if the Steering Committee didn't like the evaluation plan, hadn't read it, or wanted something else. They offered no comments and answered none of my emails. After asking the regional and local staff and not getting an answer, I called the in-house evaluator at headquarters to see if the timing of the evaluation was an issue. He assured me that the timing was good. It felt weird though, like something was wrong but I couldn't figure out what.

I sought advice from my senior advisors, who suggested that sometimes you just have to go to a place to see what is really going on before you can even begin to plan an evaluation. Being present, in person, might be the only way to get the work done. I made this case to the in-house evaluator, who agreed. A week later, I got on an airplane to complete the evaluation plan from the field and do several weeks of fieldwork.

It crossed my mind much later that getting on the airplane was a turning point. Until then, I had the option of heeding the red flags and leaving the project, but I was reluctant to do so. I had turned down other work in order to do this evaluation, and I had bills to pay. Doing this evaluation well would give me something interesting to share at conferences and, more importantly, would likely qualify me for more work elsewhere. My nagging doubts were overruled by the unfortunate combination of mortgage payments, naïve optimism, collegial encouragement, and a touch of self-interest.

To my surprise, I got off the airplane to learn that the in-country program lead had already met twice with my local colleague in the prior week, without me, the evaluation lead. To this day, I still have no idea what they discussed. I found out about these meetings in an email sent to me and copied to everyone else—Steering Committee and local staff alike—while I was in the air. Not only that, my local colleague had quit the project! She offered several reasons, but none made any sense. By the time I was able to get online and read all this in her email, it was twenty minutes before she and I were scheduled to meet the in-country staff. I went to the meeting alone.

There I was, in-country and about to start an evaluation with only a vague evaluation plan, little stakeholder input, an unresponsive Steering Committee, and now no local language skills! I had arrived, promptly lost a team member, and then had an introductory meeting with program staff immediately thereafter. This was the most progress on the evaluation since they awarded me the contract, and it was already Day 1 of the field research. I remember feeling quite alone with the overwhelming sensation of standing on very unstable terrain.

Unfortunately, the Steering Committee had a high-quality freak-out over my local colleague's email before I could reach them. Losing her (half of the field research team) threw them for a loop, as her local knowledge and language skills were important considerations when we were awarded the contract.

On Day 2, I met early with my (former) local colleague to find out what happened. Over some instant coffee, she admitted that quitting via email "might be" unprofessional and that copying the whole Steering Committee and all the local staff without speaking to me first was indeed "problematic." Even worse, I could not cajole any more information from her as to what the real problems were. She left. I swore.

I needed to figure out what to do. I called the organization's in-house evaluator back in North America. As we talked, I realized I couldn't justify pulling the plug and walking away despite my unease. The organization had its own internal reasons why they did not want to start over with the evaluation. I was sure that I wasn't the source of the problem, but I was the one standing there holding the problem. That wasn't the reputation I wanted—evaluator shows up, wrecks the place, then leaves.

What's more, when I met with the organization's local staff on Day 1, they were excited about the evaluation. They were committed professionals who legitimately wanted to know what worked well and how to improve what did not. They were prepared to act as translators, develop tools, collect and analyse data. I told the in-house evaluator as much. I decided to throw myself into the evaluation to pull something good out of it. I convinced myself and then the in-house evaluator that it was salvageable, and we agreed it should go ahead. We came up with a plan. I would deal with any in-country concerns and logistical challenges, while he dealt with the Steering Committee in North America.

From the outset of the field research, I witnessed some serious dysfunction within the organization. Personnel from one faith group were told not to express their faith while in the office, whereas others faced no such restrictions. (*Is this why I observed some very real cleavages within the staff?*) Some wanted to know why the evaluation was scheduled during planting season. (*During what? Didn't I already ask about timing?*) Other staff confided in me that they'd been warned that the new in-country program lead was untrustworthy. Conflicts small and large were frequent. Meanwhile, the in-country program lead flip-flopped on so many things that it was hard for me to keep track of what she'd said and what might be true. At one point, in her most exhausted state, she confided that she was receiving unclear and contradictory expectations about the program and the evaluation from both the regional program head and from headquarters and that she really felt abandoned. My heart went out to her, but the way she was dealing with it was pitting the staff against each other. There was no trust within the organization. (*Is this why my local colleague quit?*)

Whether or not the organization was well managed was outside the evaluation's terms of reference. Nonetheless, it was clearly a problem impacting the evaluation. I contacted my senior advisors back home, and they suggested various ways to broach the topic with the organization's in-house evaluator back at headquarters in North America. I opted for what is now my default strategy: in case of emergency be plainly, brutally honest.

The in-house evaluator listened, questioned, and asked for examples of anything I'd witnessed. He committed to dealing with it within headquarters and following up with the in-country program lead, but only after the fieldwork was complete. The evaluation continued amidst the apparent organizational dysfunction.

As the evaluation progressed, all the local staff participated, each telling me they valued the process as much as the findings. There was a day-long debrief and discussion in-country that went better than I expected, particularly given the lack of internal trust I'd seen. Staff and the in-country program lead began to plan changes to the program they could implement locally, and they put together a list of ideas for headquarters to implement more widely. These were the backbone of my recommendations. Despite the organizational mess and the rough start, I felt better. The evaluation was being used. (*Hooray!*)

Ten days later, I was back home in my own office on a call to discuss the results with the Steering Committee. The conversation turned to one of the more mundane findings. This issue was raised by a significant minority of interviewees, and several had offered the same, seemingly straightforward solution. Suddenly, the regional program head began to scream, "WHO SAID THAT? I WANT THEIR NAMES!" I couldn't have been more confused. I thought, "Well, for one, you did!" but of course I couldn't say that. I reminded everyone that confidential data collection meant I wasn't about to give out names. The screamer wasn't happy.

The draft final report came back from headquarters covered with mark-ups, questions, and changes to the findings, recommendations, and even interviewee quotes. There were even changes to items previously agreed upon by the Steering Committee. What was enthusiastically embraced and used in-country was being ferociously denied by headquarters.

Then, I received a call from a latecomer I hadn't yet met in this saga. She was one of the most experienced staff members at headquarters, just returning from extended leave. She had read the draft evaluation findings and told me, in her words, that I was "on the money." She then told me this wasn't the organization's first evaluation as I had been led to believe, but actually their third or possibly fourth. These previous evaluations had found similar results in different program locations, including the seemingly mundane issue at the centre of all the screaming.

This new piece of information took some time to process. (*Why hadn't I been told this? Had I been naïve? Was my relative inexperience one of the reasons we won the bid? Did the client think I wouldn't find the same issues? Would they ignore this evaluation, too?*)

After another long consult with my senior advisors, I sent headquarters a detailed rebuttal and an amended draft. I returned the quotes to their original wording, added more context, and re-explained portions of the methodology. I included a note reminding the Steering Committee they had approved both the plan and tools that I, the in-country manager, and local staff had developed during the first few days of the fieldwork and that they had seen findings from the field weekly.

From that point on, every detail, fact, finding, and comma in the report was questioned by the Steering Committee. They no longer met with me "for logistical reasons" but had the in-house evaluator ask me directly for changes beyond the contentious issue. I added still more context, included some of their ideas on the analyses, and made other changes I felt still reflected the data collected in the field. After a dozen conversations, I submitted an amended report. They chose not to release it.

This was a Voldemort evaluation. It was wracked with confusion, distrust, naïveté, incomplete information, and more than one lie. It was also the most exhausting evaluation in which I've ever been involved. I've never learned more from an evaluation and I'm still not certain I fully understand all the places where it went wrong.

## LESSONS LEARNED

- **Know the organization and their motivations.** This was the first big red flag I missed. Remember how the regional program head was distractingly enthusiastic about sharing the evaluation results with potential funders? I now wonder if the in-house evaluator was nervous because he knew that the evaluation was really meant to be an advertorial. I failed to accurately diagnose their motivations for the evaluation.

- **Determine if there were prior evaluations and what they said.** The latecomer in this story, the experienced person from headquarters, told me about prior evaluations but, for reasons unknown to me, did not choose to share them with me. I later found two of them, but I should have looked earlier. In them I found similar results, including the one at the centre of all the screaming. In hindsight, I would have asked whether and how the prior evaluations were implemented and possibly used some of their data collection tools.

- **Don't get on an airplane if it feels wrong.** I was uneasy getting on the airplane. I should have trusted that feeling. I should have had more conversations with the Steering Committee and gotten more information from headquarters about what was going on within the regional office and in-country first. Going there to sort out the evaluation sounded like good advice at the time, but it's not how I do things now.

- **It's okay to abandon a project.** I could have walked away from this project more than once, but I never saw that as a real option, more like something to be avoided. My mistake.

## REFLECTIVE QUESTIONS

1. How many people were new in their roles in this evaluation? How might this have impacted the evaluation?

2. What other red flags do you see in the evaluation besides the ones mentioned? Would you have walked away from this evaluation? If so, when? If not, how would you have addressed the issues raised?

3. How did the evaluator's own self-interest affect her decisions made around this evaluation?

# 22

## THE ONLY WAY OUT IS THROUGH

Melissa Al-Azzawi

### Stephanie Evergreen

*Stephanie Evergreen, PhD, is best known for being an approachable and research-based data visualization nerd.*

have failed so many times, I'm like a fail hoarder. I have failed in delivering use-ful external evaluation reports to clients. I have failed and brought others down with me in team evaluation projects. I have failed to the point that people I had gone through graduate school admiring have since shamed my work. I have failed so much that others confess their failures to me. I now collect failures like a Girl Scout with a sash full of badges.

# ABOUT ME

I am Stephanie Evergreen. I have a PhD in evaluation, though I focus most of my efforts these days on teaching my fellow data nerds how to present their data effectively. I have written several books on this topic and have a popular blog.

But I didn't start with so much leadership or enthusiasm.

I used to have a lot of FOFU.

Fear Of F-ing Up. You may have it yourself.

But like most fears, the best way out is through.

Believe it or not, even though I now speak regularly in front of hundreds of people without breaking a sweat, I used to have a fear of public speaking. In my first presentations about how to give good presentations, my hands would shake and my knees would knock behind the podium. The only way to smooth out those tremors was to keep getting up on stage.

Getting over FOFU follows the same philosophy. Once you start f-ing up, you have to just keep on f-ing up. Your first few might knock you down for a day or so, but just keep f-ing up, learn the lessons each f-up will teach you, and soon enough it'll become just a regular part of your day. I've f-ed up three times already today and it's only 12:35 pm.

I've f-ed up so much I have an entire journey to share with you.

# THE MISTAKE OR CHALLENGE

Before I knew what I was doing with data visualization and design, I was making stuff like Figure 22.1 all the time. Back in those days I was using default Microsoft Office colors to design what I thought were pretty awesome slideshows for clients. I know now that my attempts to be colorful actually generated a terrible slide. When we use dark text on a dark background like this, we make it difficult to read.

But beyond that, there's really nothing enticing or memorable about this slide. I show it in my workshops all the time to highlight what bad design looks like. Recently, as I was showing the slide (Figure 22.1), I realized my client, the person who originally hired me to prepare this slide, was in the audience. I was so embarrassed. She told me afterward, "Don't worry, Stephanie, I don't even remember those slides."

And that's exactly the point. If we want our work to have a lasting impact, it can't look like this.

**FIGURE 22.1**

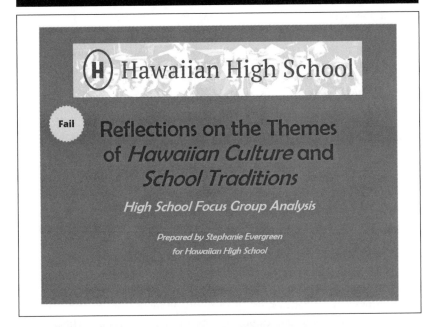

**FIGURE 22.2**

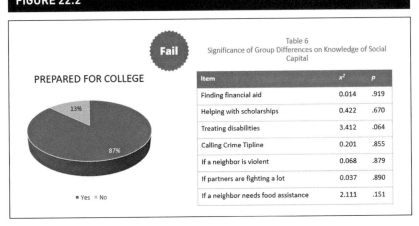

I also co-wrote evaluation reports in which I included three-dimensional (3D) pie charts. We wove in tables of chi square values, as if our audience even cared or knew what that meant (Figure 22.2).

This design was so bad, our client had to give our evaluation report to a graphic design firm, who did what they could to turn it into something the client could actually distribute to their primary audiences. However, because most graphic design firms do not know how to communicate data effectively, the resulting version of the report did not include any actual data beyond the financial status of the program, a component that was not even part of our evaluation. Looking back now, this was a compound failure that started with bad communication on our part and ended up as an unused evaluation.

Up to this point in my journey, none of these design failures bothered me because I didn't even know I was making them. It was only in hindsight, after doing deep dives into the research about data visualization and design, that I realized I had made some big mistakes.

The more I started learning about design and talking about how to present our data effectively, the more others started to share their designs (and design failures) with me.

One of my favorites was a well-intentioned map of individuals living in poverty in the Twin Cities (Minneapolis/St. Paul, Minnesota) area. There, like many places in the United States, income is closely correlated with race. The map essentially showed the distribution of poor African Americans, each represented by a red dot. The well-intentioned researchers then shared the map with the actual citizens via community meetings, where the citizens rightly complained that the map made them look like a rash on the Twin Cities.

We can all learn from this failure. In Western cultures, red is commonly associated with danger or anger. Or a rash! Be mindful of those cultural associations with specific colors, especially when visualizing at an individual level.

I continued to get better at design, working on more sophisticated products, which introduced more opportunities for other things to fail, like technology.

I once used what I thought was a helpful Excel plug-in to create awesome overlapping bar charts for one of my clients. We showcased our amazing dashboards containing these overlapping bar charts on blogs, in conference presentations, and in books.

A year passed and it was time to update the dashboard, and that's when I discovered that the plug-in had broken (Figure 22.3).

**FIGURE 22.3**

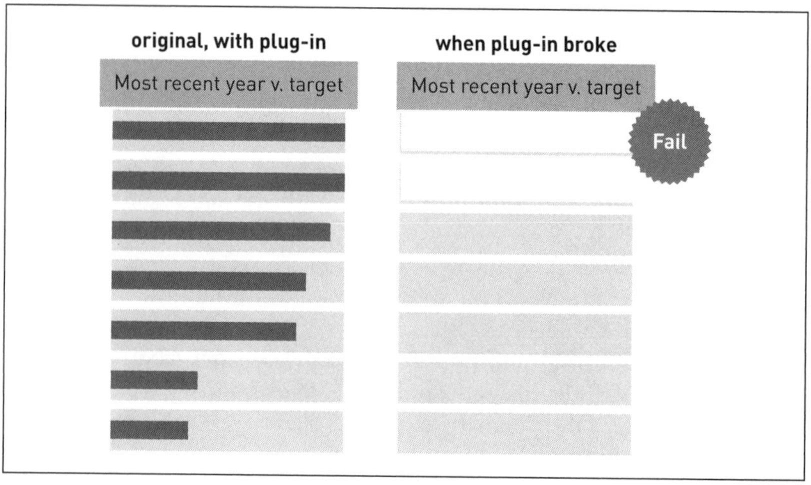

My team had to sink hours of unbillable costs into fixing this problem. We can learn from this, too. Technology is often positioned as a way to cut corners, but technology is not always reliable. Free technology, like that plug-in, is even more prone to fail because there isn't a dedicated staff to keep it updated. I should have known better than to try to cut corners.

Up to this point on my personal f-ing up journey, these failures caused headaches, inconveniences, unbillable hours, and some late nights, but that's it.

But my public profile continued to rise and, along with it, the number of people who took notice of my failures.

In my first book, somehow during the production process, several of my visuals became design failures. The printed product showed some of my visuals stretched to a point of distortion that deeply embarrassed me because my book talked about how you shouldn't do that very thing to your images (Figure 22.4).

**FIGURE 22.4**

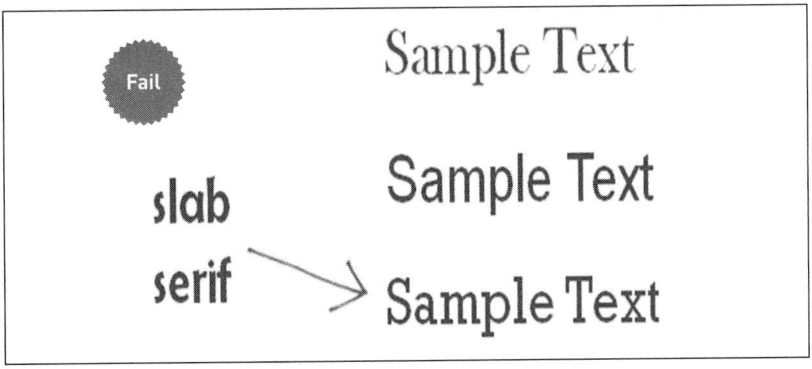

*Source:* Evergreen, Stephanie. *Presenting Data Effectively*, First Edition. Thousand Oaks, CA: SAGE Publications, Inc, 2013.

Many readers of that book also wrote to tell me that on page 100, I said RGB is best for screen and CMYK colors are best for print, but later in that chapter I had advised the exact opposite (Figure 22.5). Oops.

Unfortunately, that failure made it into print despite being reviewed many times by me, the editor, the assistant editor, the copyeditor, the proofreader, and a dozen peer reviewers.

More than a headache, these failures formed a dark cloud over my head for several days. People paid hard-earned money for the book. The mistakes were permanent. (Or so I thought. I fixed those errors in the second edition.)

The higher my profile grew, the more public my failures became. And the more public my failures became, the more people were ready and willing to point out my failures on social media, and the more I stressed out.

For example, I wrote a blog post that attempted to show three ways we can visualize when down is good. In general, we tend to interpret downward trends as bad, but there are many cases where this isn't the situation, so I tried to show ways that visualization could help shake up our ways of interpreting.

**FIGURE 22.5**

**Fail**

### Shouldn't Screen and Print Colors Match?

Chances are, if you go through this process of pulling out colors from a screenshot and adjusting your color palette in your report, when you print your report you will feel a ping of disappointment. Color rarely looks the same on paper as it does on screen, even when working with color codes. Screen monitor colors, printing ink levels, and other factors influence how well the two colors match. But, as Ware (2013) notes, precision is less important than perception. Aim to get as close as possible, without worrying about an exact match. RGB is most appropriate for things viewed on a screen. Printed materials look best with another color code, called CMYK (cyan, magenta, yellow, and black—yes, K stands for black). Both sets of color code numbers are available through most color picking tools. If you plan to print, then follow the same instructions listed here: just pop the CMYK colors into Word. However, just know that slight differences in color are such a rampant problem that it is seen as normal.

---

**KEY POINTS TO REMEMBER**

- RGB color codes are intended for things you want to print. CMYK color codes are best suited for things that appear on screen. You can translate between the two closely, but if they do not match with exactitude, don't stress out.

- Dark gray or black should always be applied to text intended for long, narrative reading. Shorter bursts of text or those less essential to comprehension can be set in different colors or can appear on a colored background.

- The default color scheme of Excel is almost never a good idea. Apply color intentionally to specific areas of the graph to communicate a point or highlight an area for greater focus.

- Color choices degrade in black-and-white print settings and regular dissemination routes. Replicate a typical distribution of your report by copying and faxing and so on to determine whether your color scheme holds up well.

*Source:* Evergreen, Stephanie. *Presenting Data Effectively*, First Edition. Thousand Oaks, CA: SAGE Publications, Inc, 2013.

**FIGURE 22.6**

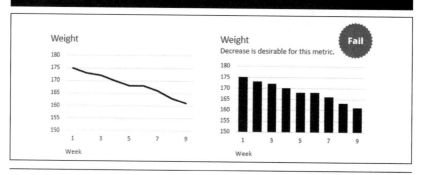

*Source:* Evergreen, Stephanie, http://stephanieevergreen.com/down-is-good/, August 12, 2015

One of my solutions was to change the chart type. Rather than showing the trend in a traditional line graph, I used a column chart (Figure 22.6). But my axis didn't start at zero. Column graphs encode data by their length and if I cut off part of the length by starting at anything other than zero, I'm messing with how brains work to interpret the data. I didn't even realize where the axis was sitting when I published the post and promoted it on social media. Soon afterward, many important people in the data visualization field jumped into the comments to correct me. The worst of all was someone considered a Godfather of data visualization, a legend, and a person you don't want to embarrass yourself in front of.

This mistake sent me into a dark corner for a day and a half. My confidence took a blow, even though this was only one tiny blog post among dozens, and I'm a twice published author with a PhD. Isn't it funny how it's so much easier to see the little failures than the big successes in life? I'm sure I'm not the only one. I could have been flattered that my blog was garnering attention from someone so well respected in data visualization, but instead I focused on my mistake and how embarrassed I was.

I learned from this incident that it is not fun to be incorrect on the internet, but when it happens, the best thing to do is issue an apology and a correction and move on. Column charts should be on an axis that starts at zero, even though this zero-axis rule is often debated as it applies to other chart types.

Many months later I published another blog post that showed ways to visualize the financials page from nonprofit and foundation board reports. Usually this data is shown as just a thick table of numbers and people tend to skip it because tables are dense and hard to work with.

I offered a redesign that used multiple small area graphs to show change in budgetary line items over a two-year period. Yet again I ventured into the y-axis debate because the scales in these area graphs did not all start at zero (Figure 22.7).

There's a solid argument to be made that the scales in these charts *shouldn't* start at zero because we wouldn't see any difference between the two years; all the lines would look flat. But there's also a solid reason why they *should* start at zero— maybe I'm exaggerating the change if I don't. Only the people who work closely with this data would know what kind of scale would fit best given the context of this foundation.

However, people once again took notice of what they thought was a failure of mine and one commenter tweeted that "there's no way [the very same Godfather who already commented on my previous blog] would approve this visual." So, I got up the guts and sent the whole thing to the Godfather himself.

The Godfather wrote back: "To be honest, almost everything about your redesign is deceitful." Ouch. I may have actually shed tears over this one. I was devastated. A couple of days later, I got another email from him. I had hoped it would reinforce my position by clarifying that there are arguments to be made on either side of this y-axis debate. But, no. He wrote: "I realized that in my last email I used the term 'deceitful' when what I actually meant was 'deceptive.'" Ouch again.

That's when I finally started to laugh about this whole failures thing. Though I appreciated the Godfather's follow-up, I was confident that my original design

FIGURE 22.7

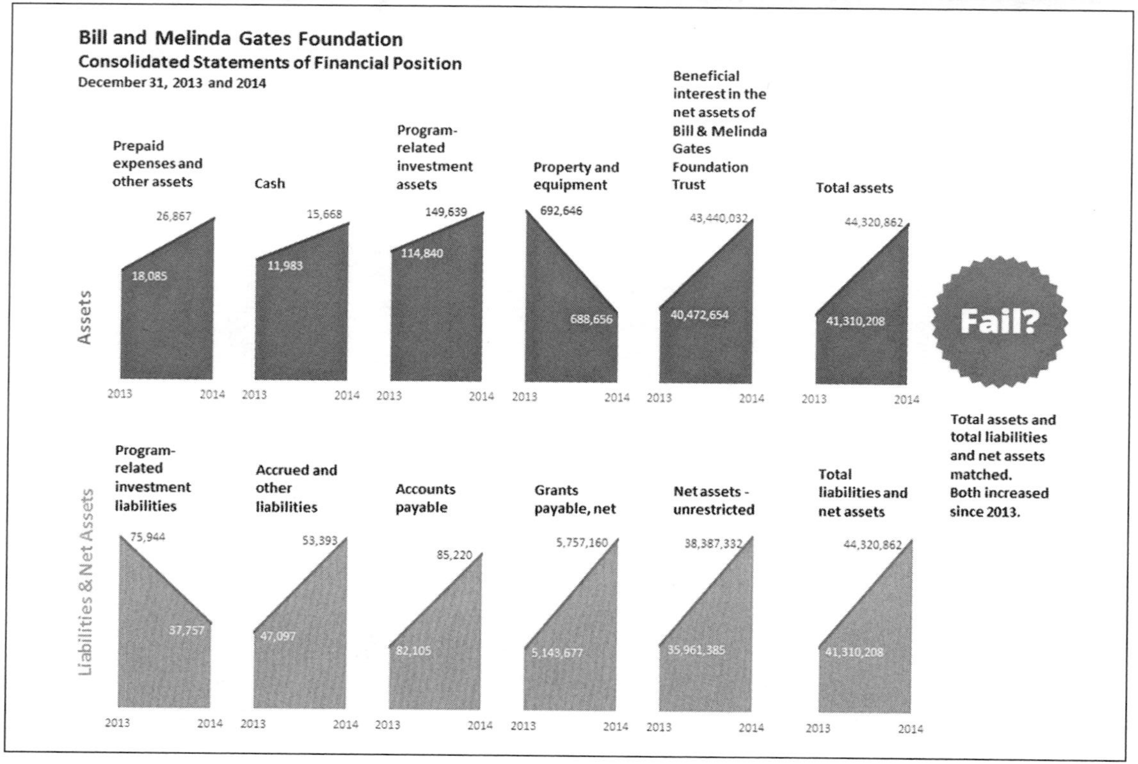

Bill and Melinda Gates Foundation
Consolidated Statements of Financial Position
December 31, 2013 and 2014

Assets

Prepaid expenses and other assets — 26,867 / 18,085

Cash — 15,668 / 11,983

Program-related investment assets — 149,639 / 114,840

Property and equipment — 692,646 / 688,656

Beneficial interest in the net assets of Bill & Melinda Gates Foundation Trust — 43,440,032 / 40,472,654

Total assets — 44,320,862 / 41,310,208

Liabilities & Net Assets

Program-related investment liabilities — 75,944 / 37,757

Accrued and other liabilities — 53,393 / 47,097

Accounts payable — 85,220 / 82,105

Grants payable, net — 5,757,160 / 5,143,677

Net assets - unrestricted — 38,387,332 / 35,961,385

Total liabilities and net assets — 44,320,862 / 41,310,208

Fail?

Total assets and total liabilities and net assets matched. Both increased since 2013.

Source: Evergreen, Stephanie, http://stephanieevergreen.com/financials/, January 6, 2016

could be justified. Experience has taught me there isn't always one "right" answer in the world of data visualization and design (except for column charts, which must always start at zero!). I legitimately felt my position had merit and that my idol was respectfully short-sighted. I wasn't in a dark corner anymore. My idol was off his pedestal.

Jana Curll

Rather than apologize, like I had done when I was actually wrong, I made the best of the situation and opened a design challenge, inviting people to contribute better visualizations of the same data. Most of the people who originally pointed out my "failure" didn't bother to participate. About a dozen people did, and the whole situation was quite collegial and fun.

A few months went by and I had long forgotten about that blog post. Then a professor emailed me to say that one of her graduate students had participated in my design challenge and she and her grad student had designed an experiment comparing my visualization to the grad student's submission. As you might have guessed, the study concluded that his version was so much better (it wasn't—he had the same scale issue that I did—but their leading questions tipped the scales in his favor). My first reaction was shock that they thought my original visualization was that bad. My second reaction was impressed that they had the guts to ask me to include my visual in their article. My third reaction was a chuckle. This is a whole new level of failure. I had moved beyond social media critics to failures that would appear in print!

## LESSONS LEARNED

In addition to the tiny lessons learned about design throughout this chapter, my failures journey also generates more complex lessons, some of which I'm still figuring out.

- **Experience is only gained through a lot of f-ing up.** Had the professor notified me that her graduate student was including my failure in his study back when I was still making 3D pie charts for evaluation reports, I think I might have quit my academic program and tried hard to make myself invisible. However, experience has given me confidence, the ability to discern nuance, and the foresight that tomorrow is another day.

- **The only way out is through.** It's taken a lot of failed designs to get where I am, but what has worked for me is to get embarrassed so often that the embarrassment stops overshadowing my ability to see clearly. Don't get me wrong, I take the criticism seriously. I see where I've failed so I know what to fix. But I don't let it break me like it used to. Now I laugh about my failures at cocktail parties.

- **Some days are better than other days.** I'd be lying to you if I ended this chapter right there. The truth of the matter is that my feelings and insights about my failures are all over the place. There are days I wish I had never started a blog because of the number of times I have had to delete comments from people trying to point out mistakes when they clearly didn't even read the whole post. There are days I blame social media for the anonymous critic culture that it has allowed us to create. There are days I feel like a total imposter, like my résumé is one failure after another and the whole world knows it.

- **FOFU has turned into ATIWFU (Acceptance That I Will F-Up. A lot. Daily.)** So long as I continue to put work out there, I'll keep having opportunities to fail. I could stay inside my shell and never offer the world anything of my own design, like many people on social media do. But I have never been one to stay quiet. My love of supporting others as they become better designers and visualizers is too strong to stop putting new ideas out there into the world. My alternative, and this might not work for everyone, has been to deal with my own issues around perfectionism so that I stop expecting my work to be flawless.

- **A social media diet can help tremendously.** There's nothing I can do about Twitter culture or internet trolls. I can manage my own expectations around failure, but I can't manage theirs. What I can do is stay off social media as much as possible. I can be sure I have a broad life with many interests and lots of love so that the failures at work are smaller in proportion. Stephanie fails, and then she goes on a bike ride.

# REFLECTIVE QUESTIONS

1. How would you handle a senior member of your field informing you that you made a serious mistake? How would you handle it if you thought that person was wrong?

2. What are some ways that evaluators can build reflective practice into their work?

3. Is there something about fearing our own failure that actually drives us toward careers like evaluation, where we're responsible for assessing others' failures? How could facing our own failures make us better evaluators?

# CONCLUSION

The stories in this book illustrate that mistakes and failures can occur at every stage of the program evaluation process. I am grateful to each and every contributor in this book for their willingness to share experiences that I suspect were likely very upsetting and stressful at the time.

Despite the uniqueness of each author's situation, the difficulties they encountered were often similar. When I first envisioned this book, I imagined that many of the failures would involve complications with data collection. Although this definitely was the case for Bisgard and Selvaggio, Noga, and Snyder, there were shared mistakes in other areas, too.

One of the most common problems experienced was having to manage the (sometimes conflicting) desires and expectations of program staff and clients. Archibald, Barrington, Bisgard and Selvaggio, Lovato, O'Reilly, Muramutsa, Newhouse, Shepherd, Steinberg, Tindall, and Williams all found themselves walking a version of Mohan's tightrope of evaluator responsiveness versus independence. Using participatory approaches and being attentive to client or stakeholder needs while also maintaining independence is a struggle we often face in this profession. Being able to communicate and negotiate both effectively and proactively are essential for navigating these occasionally rough waters.

Another common stumbling block was engaging clients and stakeholders in ways appropriate to the evaluation context. For Archibald, Lovato, Preskill, and myself, excluding certain clients and stakeholders was an oversight. For Muramutsa, it was a more challenging dilemma of balancing one stakeholder's wishes against the other. For Castillo and Igras, stakeholder complications were the result of subtle cross-cultural issues. In Steinberg's case, it was a challenging issue of trying to find a good "fit" between a group of stakeholders and oneself as the evaluator. As evaluators, we have long understood the importance of engaging stakeholders, but sometimes achieving this in practice can be more difficult than it seems.

Barrington, Davidson, Dean-Coffey, and Newhouse each had to deal with changes in scope that significantly affected their original evaluation plan. Evaluation clearly does not occur in a static environment. However, it is usually necessary to define the scope of an evaluation at the outset and develop some form of an evaluation plan. Although the advent of developmental evaluation provides us with a more flexible approach, it is important to note that even Michael Quinn Patton acknowledges that it is not an appropriate method for all evaluation scenarios. In addition, the rigid procurement process of many organizations often discourages the use of developmental evaluation. Finding the balance between planning for an evaluation while also remaining fluid and responsive to inevitable changes, all within budget, will continue to be a delicate task for evaluators, particularly external ones. Suggested safeguards such as shorter term contracts, contingency budgets, and timeline buffers are very useful options to consider.

Barrington, Davidson, Dean-Coffey, and O'Reilly experienced unexpected turnover in program management and other personnel that negatively affected the progress of the evaluation. In retrospect, these changes were usually a major warning sign to the evaluator. Although we cannot always predict these events, we can learn to at least expect them and be prepared to spend the extra time required to orient new personnel to the evaluation.

Finally, Barrington, Bisgard and Selvaggio, Castillo, Gauthier, Igras, O'Reilly, and Tindall realized the important role that context plays in informing all aspects of an evaluation. Equally important, Evergreen learned to embrace her failures and develop a thicker skin.

Although many of the authors' lessons learned are situation-specific, several common themes emerge across chapters.

It is probably no surprise that many of the lessons learned emphasize the importance of engaging clients and stakeholders appropriately at multiple points in the evaluation. Even when you think you have, maybe you actually haven't. Castillo reminds us to engage all stakeholders in the development of data collection instruments, and Preskill and Tindall advocate for participatory data analysis parties. Both of the stories from Lovato and myself remind us that when developing items such as logic models and system maps, it is the people and the process that are more important than the product.

Another lesson is the need to reflect on the context of a program and its evaluation. Barrington, Gauthier, and Tindall now view programs as part of a larger and constantly changing context that can strongly influence an evaluation. Castillo notes you can have small local contexts within larger program contexts. Igras advises evaluators to research the political, social, and historical context of a country to better engage stakeholders. O'Reilly recommends understanding more clearly the context behind an organization's motivation for evaluation. Finally, Mohan and Newhouse suggest we take some time to walk in the shoes of our clients and stakeholders to better understand how their reality can influence the course of an evaluation project.

Many of the stories told underscore the need for evaluators to communicate effectively. Excellent communication is instrumental for managing and aligning expectations, troubleshooting minor issues, and building trusting relationships. Archibald now listens to his instincts and communicates any concerns immediately. Barrington ensures she has a direct line of communication with key stakeholders. Mohan uses communication to double-check his assumptions and to surface any potential problems.

For O'Reilly, Shepherd, and Snyder, perhaps the hardest lesson for any evaluator was learning to trust their instincts and know when to pull the plug on an evaluation.

Avoiding these failures and judgement errors often requires the "soft" skills of evaluation, such as interpersonal skills, effective communication, negotiation, and self-care. There is definitely more to being an evaluator than simply mastering the technical skills. Unfortunately, soft skills cannot always be taught in a classroom. They often come from experience, and occasionally that experience is negative. However, trusted mentors can play a valuable role in assisting new evaluators as they find their way.

Virtually all evaluations will face setbacks of one kind or another. Some will have more than others, and some are more serious than others, but most do not end up as epic failures. And not all failure is a bad thing. The most valuable lessons come from our mistakes, which over time inform better practice, as awkward as they may have been at the time. For example, Lovato's failure to engage an important stakeholder initiated a process that resulted in a stronger relationship overall.

Reading this book will not make you immune to failure or blunders, but hopefully, learning from others will make you more comfortable with the fact that mistakes occur. We are often our own toughest critics, especially with the benefit of 20/20 hindsight. But even the most experienced evaluators are prone to errors, and they have become better practitioners as a result.

Change happens, and evaluators cannot anticipate or control everything in an evaluation project. But we can learn to expect the unexpected. If there is an antidote to failure, it is having a strong reflective practice that helps us to identify and manage minor challenges before they turn into full-blown blunders. The need for reflection surfaces again and again in these stories. As Williams advised, if you are struggling with self-reflection, seek the advice of mentors and colleagues who have likely wrestled with similar issues.

As reflective evaluators, we are always learning. In fact, since starting this book over a year ago, I have experienced at least one new bungle that I am still processing. I am sure I'm not alone.

When you are ready, I invite you to come and join us. Take your failures out of the closet and wear them proudly so that others can learn from them. It is our responsibility as evaluators to lead by example.

Kylie Hutchinson
Editor